James Hoehn

Illustrated JAGUAR BUYER'S GUIDE T.M.

Motorbooks International ®
Publishers & Wholesalers Inc.
Osceola, Wisconsin 54020, USA

First published in 1984 by Motorbooks International Publishers
& Wholesalers Inc, PO Box 2, 729 Prospect Avenue, Osceola, WI
54020 USA

Printed and bound in the United States of America

Library of Congress Cataloging-in-Publication Data

Hoehn, James
    Illustrated Jaguar buyer's guide.

    Bibliography: p.
    1. Jaguar automobile—Purchasing.   I. Title.
TL215.J3H64 1987   629.2′222   87-18657
ISBN 0-87938-275-9 (pbk.)

ACKNOWLEDGMENTS

In the medical field, there is an adage that "The presentor learns more from preparation for his presentation than do those who receive the presentation." The adage certainly holds true for this monograph. The digging for facts and photographs only heightened my enthusiasm and increased my understanding. Jaguar owners are a "proud" bunch and always seem willing to either discuss or show their cars. A large number of these enthusiasts have contributed to the success of this venture—some willingly and many without knowing.

None of this is truly possible without help. My thanks to all Jaguar enthusiasts who have aided and abetted this book. Specific thanks are owed to Andrew Whyte, Michael Cook at Jaguar Cars, William Kimberley of Dalton Watson Publishers, John Rupp and the editorial staff at Motorbooks International.

The future holds promise for new and exciting models from Jaguar Cars, Ltd. As we go to press, the rumors of the XJ-40 are rampant and we hope to see it soon. The fall of 1983 saw the introduction of the XJ-S cabriolet. It, unfortunately, is a rather half-hearted attempt to produce a convertible on the XJ-S theme. It approaches the drop-head coupe and the laundaulette in that the top remains rigid but the natural lines are actually spoiled by the cross-bows. The total effect is that of an XJ-S with the sheet metal off but the top frame structure in place. Something better cannot be far behind.

The world of Jaguar lovers is constantly awash with rumors of new models. These rumors were recently reignited by *Motor Trend*'s report that the design engineers were working with a concept developed by Pinin Farina in 1978. The street-word labels the new car, the offspring of the E-Type, the XK-F. It is slated for 1986.

PREFACE TO THE SECOND EDITION

"Anticipation is often greater than the satisfaction," so said a wise but unnamed philosopher. However, in the current instance, the new Jaguar XJ6 sedan is worth the wait. The first models are just arriving as I prepare this edition for press and thus included is a new section on it as well as on the XJ-SC and custom-built, but factory-offered XJ-S convertible.

John Egan, the successor to Sir William Lyons, refused to confirm or deny the rumors of either a new sports model (the now legendary XKF) or a new smaller sports saloon.

Regretably, the spirit, mover, founder and designer of Jaguars, Sir William Lyons, is no longer with us. The tributes and immortalization of his contributions had begun before his death and his spirit will live in the beauty of his cars and the hearts of their collectors.

In addition to the acknowledgements noted in the first edition, I owe a debt of gratitude to Jack Rabell, among many, who offered constructive criticism, both professional and otherwise.

TABLE OF CONTENTS

INVESTMENT RATING

Any attempt to rate automobiles for investment purposes must account for many factors. The most assessable factors are styling, performance and condition. Perhaps, in a simplistic fashion, these three factors may be equated:

I.D. (investment desirability) = style times performance divided by condition. The numerators of this equation are obvious; the denominator is not. Perhaps the solution to assessment of model designation (style) and the evaluation of condition are the moving factors behind this book.

Assessment of condition is difficult for the novice but some guidelines are available. The Antique Automobile Club of America, The Classic Car Club of America, The Contemporary Historical Vehicle Club of America and The Milestone Car Society have developed rating forms for use in concours competitions. Although no one of them is absolute (each is a bit personal and designed to meet the needs of its organization), they do itemize a reference list for automotive condition assessment. Based on this information and coordinated with the general ranking of Jaguars for investment desirability, the following rating system is offered:

★★★★★ Most Desirable. Styling and/or engineering are memorable. Is usually rare but always recognizable—e.g. SS 100. These cars usually appreciate in price.

★★★★ Desirable. Includes cars which may be close to those above but which have styling elements and/or mechanical designs which were subsequently improved.

★★★ Average. These cars are what the word says, average—in styling, mechanics or condition. These cars will not move up to the Desirable class even with a perfect restoration.

★★ Below Average. These cars are obvious in their flaws. The novice will not have a great problem identifying these vehicles.

★ Undesirable. Although uncommon, every manufacturer occasionally produced a lemon.

INTRODUCTION

For almost five decades, Sir William Lyons influenced sports (personal) automotive styling. If one includes the early efforts of the Swallow Sidecar Company, Ltd., the span approaches sixty years. Chances are good that you, as I, can recall an XK 120 roadster purring down a tree-shaded lane. The desire ignited then may really only be satiated by the pride of ownership. This book is created to ease the pains of satisfying your desire.

Acquiring a Jaguar may be a studied and reasoned action or it may be, and frequently is, an impulsive act. In either event, consideration of a number of factors may make the experience of buying, restoring, driving or showing your Jaguar more rewarding.

Research. Investigating and learning about your prospective Jaguar will enhance your pleasure. Extensive research and colorful authorship have characterized the books which have appeared in the last decade. Paul Skilleter, Andrew Whyte, Michael Frostick, Chris Harvey and Lord Montagu, to name but a few, have provided volumes of information which can enhance one's technical knowledge. A noninclusive but helpful bibliography is included at the end of this book.

Locating a Seller. Finding a Jaguar for sale is not difficult. Finding *the* Jaguar may be very difficult. *E-Jag*, a national magazine devoted originally to the New England E-type owner but now expanded to all Jaguars and all areas of the country, has an extensive want-ad section in its monthly editions and would be a good place to start. Also offering a moderate selection of used Jaguars at a variety of prices are *Road & Track* and *Hemmings Motor News* (an entire magazine of automotive want-ads).

Checking your local newspaper may be helpful if you live close to a large metropolitan area. For example, *The New York Times* and the *Los Angeles Times* are newspapers with specific want-ad sections for antique, classic and special interest cars as well as late model cars with special groupings for Jaguar.

A word of caution to the ad reader: A level of credibility can be established by considering the source of the advertisement. The potential buyer should read about and then look critically at any potential Jaguar for purchase—what you read is not always what you see or what you buy. For example, one must be wary of general newspaper ads, but can expect reasonable accuracy from those in *E-Jag*. Where doubt or ignorance exists, consult an expert. One fast way to become a knowledgeable buyer is to read many want ads and see many cars. You'll rapidly learn what the phrases "needs a little work to show" and "recent partial restoration" mean. Again, consult an expert when in doubt.

Traveling to Great Britain or the Continent in hopes of finding a bargain car may be a good excuse for a European vacation, but beware of the United States government regulations regarding importation of cars. It would be wise to know beforehand the cost of any modifications needed to import and register a car. However, some of the prewar and early postwar Jaguars are more common in Great Britain and may be exempt from federal emission control standards. Check the current laws before you buy your airplane ticket. Remember, if you choose this method of acquiring a late model Jaguar, it must be certifiable by the US government before you drive the first mile.

A word about "gray-market" cars is in order. When the US dollar rose to such great strength against the English Pound Sterling, a dollar bought an awful lot of European auto. The English and European markets were literally raided for late-model, used Mercedes-Benz cars. Inevitably, "home-production" Jaguars began to arrive in the United States. The company was concerned because "home" cars are not manufactured to the tougher US specifications and the conversions are frequently incomplete. Thus, Jaguar Cars will refuse to honor any remaining warranty on "gray-market" cars. However, with the fall of the dollar in early 1987, the market became no longer significantly profitable.

Personal Considerations. Many Jaguars have been purchased "for a lark," which is not to be condemned out of hand, but which has frequently proven costly for the buyer. If you can determine your own motives (for example, investment versus transportation), your choice of a Jaguar model may become much easier.

If you are purchasing for investment, you should consider your concern for originality. Restoration can be an expensive proposition requiring substantial "up-front" money. Restoring to original condition with original parts can be prohibitive. However, certifiable originality will bring the highest returns in the seller's market of classic automobile auctions.

The same consideration should be given to any car which has been significantly modified. Jaguar has not manufactured any V-8 engines but Daimler has (their distinguishing features will be discussed later). Several professional conversions to "American reliability" exist. Acceptance of such a situation may provide better performance and ease of maintenance, but is a poor investment for originality.

Area Considerations. The climate of your driving area should be considered. Some Jaguars have tops and side windows which have a marked propensity to leak. Thus, if one lived in the Northwest coastal areas, the choice of a fixed-head coupe might be wiser than a roadster. If you wish to provide elegant family transportation, the wide variety of Jaguar sedans will allow a choice to fit most budgets. Also, early Jaguar models which are driven consistently in warm or hot climates should be modified with overflow tanks lest boilovers become a significant problem.

You should also research the local availability of Jaguar parts and repair service. Jaguar (and later British Leyland, [BL,] and Jaguar-Rover-Triumph, [JRT]) has offered factory training for mechanics. Most major metropolitan areas can claim at least one dealership with a competent mechanic. However, the best Jaguar mechanic may not be affiliated with the local Jaguar dealership so it pays to ask other Jaguar owners for their recommendations.

Cost Considerations. Labor costs for the mechanical services will vary from locale to locale, but should, in general, approximate hourly costs for American or standard foreign car repair work. As you get more familiar with your Jaguar, you may wish to acquire a shop manual for your particular model and perform routine maintenance and minor repairs yourself. This progressive involvement is part of the enjoyment of owning your Jaguar.

Parts availability will depend on car age and part requirement. Cost for original parts versus reproduction parts may vary considerably. However, reproduction parts may be the only ones available. Mechanical parts are relatively easy to find as engine and drivetrain designs have remained relatively constant through the years. Body replacement parts may present more of a problem. One needs only to read the wanted sections of most Jaguar publications to understand the magnitude of the shortage. There are, however, several large auto salvage operations which specialize in British autos and a few which deal solely in Jaguar parts (see appendix).

Restoration shops that specialize in Jaguars are available but their waiting lines are long. Many restorers would like to "do your car" but the Jaguar enthusiast is advised to research a body restoration shop by consulting other Jaguar owners who have used the particular service and look at multiple examples of its finished work. Any restoration service good enough to do your car should be proud enough of its work to suggest endorsements.

You should consider the type of restorative work you wish. If you want the Jaguar to look good for driving around town, then the local body shop may be able to satisfy your needs under your supervision. But, if you want to enter local or regional car shows (concours), you will want a more precise restoration—the competition will get tighter and the scrutiny even keener at national events. Events held by local Jaguar clubs are often educational events to be entered by the novice, and even major JCNA events will have most top-rated cars restored by their owners. It should be pointed out here that many of these owners possess skills that are tantamount to professional restorers. *But* they restore for love rather than money. Open national events, such as sponsored by the CCCA, usually require professional restorations to be competitive. The production of a "100-point" car is an undertaking of great magnitude and should be avoided by anyone on a shoestring budget. A certifiable restoration will usually run well into five figures before completion. Obviously, however, the best investment protection lies in this category.

As you shop for an appropriate Jaguar, you will find that most of the SS 100's have been totally (or near-totally) restored and the purchase prices will reflect that cost as well as their desirability. On the other hand, XK 120, 140 and 150 models, as well as most of the postwar sedans, are available for restoration.

Local Enthusiasm. Enjoyment of your Jaguar can be enhanced by participation in a local club or group (see appendix). Most areas have a group and most are affiliated with Jaguar Clubs of North America (JCNA). Again, ask around. Most Jaguar owners will respond to a note on a windshield asking for advice.

TIPS ON "CHECKING-OUT" A JAGUAR

After you have researched your theoretical problems (costs, labor, enthusiasm and so on), the next step is to look at a Jaguar, any Jaguar. You should be able to verify models and styles. Hopefully, further study of this book will allow you to separate the XK 120 from the XK 140 and to sort through the various styles and modifications (factory and otherwise) of the sedans. Frequently, the casual owner may not know the precise year and model he owns. This can be advantageous to the educated buyer, but can often disappoint the uninformed buyer.

Serial Number Location. The first obvious benefit of your self-education about Jaguars in general and research about the specific model at hand is being able to locate serial numbers, which (in Jaguar cars) exist for the chassis, the engine, the body and the gearbox. All are stamped on an engraved brass plate which is riveted to the firewall *in* the engine compartment. The chassis number is stamped on the left side-member (often in two locations—front and rear). This number is commonly used for car identification within a series. The engine number is duplicated on the right-hand side of the cylinder block or in the spark plug well of the cylinder head. The body number may appear stamped in the wood and/or metal frame members but these places will vary from model to model. Often, the older cars will require some exploration to find these numbers. The gearbox number is stamped on the gearbox casing on most models.

Examination of the Body. Look at the rust-sensitive areas—headlight rims, front fender body mounts, parking lights, door panels, trunk moldings and exterior sheetmetal. Also, look specifically at the seams of the hood and doors. The space surrounding the hood, doors and trunk should be equal and similar. Examine the roadster or convertible top. If it is down, put it up. The top bows should move easily. Put on the side curtains. The Plexiglas window should be clear, but older windows are often stained and/or checked by sun, humidity and age.

Next, open *all* the doors and the hood and trunk. They should open and close easily but they may not self-close and latch as on an American car. Do not overlook the light weight and delicate construction of many of the integral parts of these cars. Remember, these cars were built for the enthusiast and were intended to be loved, serviced and cared for, but not to withstand much abuse.

Snoop Around the Interior. Original seats were covered in Connolly leather hides and their condition should be assessed. Some checking and fading should be anticipated in older cars, but new leather should not be discounted as nonauthentic, as replacement covers of real Connolly hides are now available. In the drophead coupes, fixed-head coupes and the sedans, the dashboard and trim were fashioned by hand from burled walnut veneers and the condition of the wood needs to be assessed also. Even if the finish is checked and marred, the wood can usually be refinished. Original finish materials are still available. Open the dashboard compartment and all ashtrays, doors and cubbyholes. Often, small missing parts, which have been "stored" for future repair, are found here.

Now, ask the owner to start the engine. It should start readily and run smoothly at 800 to 1000 rpm once warm. If it doesn't, it is fair to ask the owner to put it in running condition. Be sure to see and drive the car again as the problem may be easily corrected.

A word of caution: If mechanical problems exist which are unsolvable, buying a car "as is" can save a lot of money. But beware! More than one problem can exist. Frequently this approach has produced unhappy owners. The uninitiated are cautioned to avoid this type of purchase.

Open the hood and watch the engine as it idles. It should be almost motionless if properly tuned. The noise of the camshaft and the chain drive is chattery but normal. A quick burst of accelerator speed will cause some engine motion and occasionally a puff of blue smoke. Although continuous exhaust smoke may mean worn-out rings, most older Jaguar engines are "loose" enough to push out more than one quart of oil during 1,000 miles of driving under normal conditions.

A word of caution about poorly tuned Jaguars: If it doesn't start easily or idle smoothly, do not despair! Carburetor adjustment (especially needed in cars stored for long periods) is easily performed. Some early 3.8 liter E-types were fitted with triple SU carburetors which are notoriously difficult to keep balanced and in adjustment. If considering purchase of such an early E-type, be sure to drive the car several times and in varying weather conditions if possible.

Road Test. Follow the visual inspection of the car and the engine with a road test, asking the owner-seller to drive the car while you stand away from it. Look and listen. The information gained here can be the most valuable regarding the personality of the car and type of use and care it has received.

Then, drive the car yourself with the owner-seller. Do not hesitate to question him or her about the car and its performance, especially those aspects which do not respond well for you.

Finally, ask to drive the car by yourself. Do not hesitate to ask to use the car for an extended period. The owner-seller who is confident of the vehicle usually will not hesitate to lend the car to a serious purchase prospect.

I wish to stress care and gentle handling, especially of someone else's older model, to avoid precipitating any failures. Thirty minutes of mixed city and open-road driving usually allows a good assessment of the car and its mechanical status.

During the solo test drive, be sure to shift the gears of both the standard and the automatic transmissions through their ranges in both directions. Remember, though, do not try to downshift from second to first gear in that beautiful white XK 120 roadster—all standard transmissions until the later E-type had no synchromesh on the second-to-first-gear downshift. If, by chance, it does downshift easily, beware of significant transmission problems or transmission replacement.

Early Jaguar standard transmissions possessed very "tight" characteristics with a short travel distance in the clutch pedal. This will take some getting used to in a car with a good transmission. If gear shifts feel more like those of a Volkswagen, clutch plate wear must be suspected.

As you drive, observe the Smith gauges. The oil pressure gauge should register a variation with engine rpm changes, but should be fairly steady with sustained speed. Be sure to drive the car long enough in city traffic to check for overheating, for which Jaguars of early vintage were famous. Overheating in the prospective car may not be an insurmountable problem, as cleaning the cooling system or an accessory water overflow tank may solve this problem. Knowledge of the history of the car may indicate that it has recently been moved from one climate to another without the requisite carburetor and cooling system adjustments. In older or high-mileage cars, overheating can also signal the need for a new thermostat which is simple to install. The battery gauge should register constantly in the center (normal) range. Turn the headlights on and note the action of the gauge needle. It should fluctuate slightly.

General Comments. Test each accessory and be sure the functions of all switches are explained and understood. Some older Jaguars have had the automatic choke mechanism bypassed with a toggle switch. In some Jaguars that I've examined, interim repairs of the electrical system have been accomplished by double-wiring techniques. This can present significant problems for the owner who wishes to restore. New wiring harnesses are readily available but difficult to install.

You should, of course, examine the tires for signs of age, wear and misalignment. Although all would be solvable problems, the cost of four sixteen-inch tires complete with inner tubes for an older model is not insignificant.

While inspecting rubber, be sure to look at window and door moldings. Replacement rubber gaskets for most models are now manufactured. Although fitting them may seem cumbersome, it is not impossible. Older models also have felt or rubber grommets between the body and the fenders (the rear fender seams of the XK 120 series, for example), which are sources of moisture retention (read rust production). Gently investigate the integrity of these pads with an ice pick or similar tool. Expect them to be old and original.

Finally, review a mental check list of the items that you have noted to be of concern. Or, you could consult the concours check list used by most organizations, as a reminder of things to watch out for.

Beware. Perhaps more true today than a decade ago, the thrill of sitting on the Connolly hides, looking out over the boat-shell fenders and listening to the "burble" of the twin cams has changed many a serious business arrangement into a love affair. If this happens to you, dollar negotiations tend to become abbreviated. But, "forewarned is forearmed." So . . . go ahead, let it happen to you. Then you'll know that special feeling that controls Jaguar owners.

CHAPTER 1
THE PREWAR CARS
1929-1940

Swallow bodies	★★★★
Swallow cars	★★★★
SS sedans	★★★★
SS drop-head coupes	★★★★★
Other SS I models	★★★★★
Other SS II models	★★★★
SS 90	★★★★★
SS 100	★★★★★

William Lyons acquired an Austin Seven in 1926 and launched a lifelong personal statement of automotive styling and design that was to affect several generations of automotive stylists and enthusiasts. His influence began with the Swallow body modifications announced in 1927 for the Austin motorcars, which offered the Englishman the "1,000-pound look" for about £275. The designs of Bill Lyons were also offered to Alvis, Fiat, Swift and Morris-Cowley by 1930. Several of these vehicles are currently thought to exist only in photographs, so acquisition of one is highly desirable. However, the collector rating is somewhat lower. Multiple variations were offered and the records of what was actually produced vary from author to author and the buyer is cautioned to research a prospective purchase with extreme care.

The Swallow Sidecar Company became the Swallow Coachbuilding Company Ltd., and produced the Standard-Swallow car in 1931. The adaptation of the "low look" of the Swallow bodies to several chassis provided the proving ground for the development of the SS cars. The design evolution is easily seen.

The engines, transmissions and chassis of these early Lyons efforts were supplied by various manufacturers. The clean design and pleasant proportions which were to be trademarks of all of Lyons' designs ensured the popularity of the products of the new Swallow Coachbuilding Company. Body design and color selections initially shown in the Austin Seven and the Swift-Swallow were expanded and became available subsequently in the Fiat-Swallow and the Wolseley-Hornet. They all previewed the styling of the new SS I and II, which followed in 1932. The "long, low look" as it was called by Robert Henly, an early British distributor, implied power. These early styling efforts were instantaneously and immensely popular.

Recognition of all the Swallow bodies lies in the vertical bar present in the grille. Most cars produced were finished in a two-tone color combination featuring carnation red or apple green on the top and a rich cream on the bottom. A few cars were

An early Austin Seven with body by Swallow
Sidecars Ltd. Michael Frostick photo.

A Swift 10 equipped with a Swallow body. Although the size is
obviously different, the similarity is striking. Michael Frostick
photo.

A 1930 Austin Swallow drop-head convertible. Michael Frostick
photo.

delivered with the contrasting colors only on the bicycle fenders (wings) and the belt-line color stripe. And, to confuse the issue, some were produced totally in black. The Swallow interiors were generally far more luxurious than those offered by the original manufacturer and were completed in embossed leather. When one reflects on the fact that this added luxury cost the consumer only £15 or £20 more, it is no wonder that the Swallow Coach-building Company was besieged with orders.

Although the total number of Swallow bodies produced is unknown, several estimations are available. From serial numbers (on the door panels), it is believed that approximately 3,500 Austin-Swallows were produced. When this figure is increased by the indistinct and obscure production numbers available for the Swallow contributions on Morris-Cowley, Fiat, Swift (thought to be around 100) and Standard chassis (approximately fifty-three), the total production for the years 1929 through 1932 may approach 3,750.

Morris introduced the Wolseley-Hornet in 1931, and soon thereafter this six-cylinder two-seater became the chassis for most of the Swallow production (approximately 325). In 1932, the Wolseley-Hornet Special was produced in chassis-only form. Special features included twin SU carburetors and a four-speed gearbox. Many of the Swallows of this era were hallmarked by a "ship's scuttle" external ventilator mounted on the hood. Double bumpers, center-lock wire wheels and bright color schemes were additional optional trademarks.

In 1932, Lyons and the now-established works in Coventry limited their production almost entirely to the Wolseley-Hornet chassis and began the next phase of growth—the production of an entire automobile.

All of these special-production bodies are truly antiques and collector items by virtue of their rarity, and acquisition will be difficult. Restoration will be mostly by hand but will afford a satisfying, educational and profitable venture.

The first cars with thoroughly Jaguar lineage were the SS models introduced late in 1931. The origins of the design and style leave little doubt when one compares the design of the Swallow cars before them.

SS I

The fixed-head, or coupe model, which was introduced in October 1931 was offered in two versions: the Sixteen (2054 cc) and the Twenty (2552 cc). Both possessed engines and chassis produced by Standard.

Revisions in styling and engineering were made yearly and are commonly called model year changes now. The 1933 "first revision" styling changes smoothed the exterior appearance by lengthening the body (probably for the comfort of the passengers

A second-generation Swallow body mounted on an Austin Seven. This model is distinguished by the vertical bar in the radiator grille. Lord Montagu of Beaulieu photo.

SWALLOW CARS

ENGINE

Type: dependent on chassis and drivetrain. Most were 4-cylinder engines that displaced between 747 and 1500 cc. Later models were equipped with 6 cylinders and ranged up to 2000 cc.

Bore x Stroke, mm: 65x106

Displacement: 2054 cc or 2552 cc (1931), 2943 cc or 2663 cc (1933)

Valve Operation: side-valve

Compression Ratio: variable, depending on engine

Carburetion: single SU or RAG

Bhp (Mrf): 53-68 @ approx. 4000 rpm

CHASSIS & DRIVETRAIN

Transmission: 4-speed standard (synchromesh was added in second, third and fourth gears in 1934)

Rear Suspension: Standard production with silent bloc and spring shackles

Gear Ratio: 4.66:1

Front Suspension: Standard production

Frame: double-dropped frame produced by Standard, bracing was added in 1934

GENERAL

Wheelbase, inches: 112, 117 (1933)

Track, inches: 49, 51 (1933), 53 (1934)

Brakes: 12.5 wide Bendix draw

Tire Size, front and rear: 6.00x16

Wheels: Ragland wire-center knock-off

Body Builder: several (see text)

Chassis Serial numbers: varied according to the manufacturer of the chassis. Records are spotty.

Early SS I. Note the longer body and lower profile on this closed model. Author collection.

enclosed in the "rear seat") and removing the fender tie bar beneath the headlights. The radiator maintained its characteristic dividing bar and the curved interior margins first seen in the Standard-Swallows.

The tourer model was added in 1933, which provided the rear passenger with better vision through side windows. This design was to be continued for the remainder of the production run. In 1934-35, a sedan (called saloon in England) was added.

The second revision appeared in 1934-35. Design improvements included a new radiator shell and the hexagonal SS marque medallion. This shape appeared also on the dashboard, as an ornamental edge design for the gauges.

In 1935, two additional cars were introduced: the Airline saloon and the SS 90. The latter was of such impact and interest that it will be covered in a separate section. The Airline saloon introduced a new concept in external styling, no doubt induced in part by the avant-garde designs appearing in the US from the drawing boards of Gordon Buehrig and others. Its style became an immediate success and the production numbers indicate its popularity—approximately twenty-five percent of the entire 1934-35 production, which totaled about 4,250 units.

In 1935, the drop-head coupe was introduced. This four-seater of beautiful proportions has been claimed by some thoughtful observers to be one of the best designs that William Lyons produced. Its long hood lines and balanced grace foretold the design traits of Jaguar cars from the SS 100 through the XK 120, XK-E, even to the XJ-S introduced in 1975. Unfortunately, only ninety-four were produced in the 1935 production run and six in 1936, according to Andrew Whyte in his book, *Jaguar: The History of a Great British Car*, and few are seen today. Intriguing features were introduced in the drop-head model. The storage compartment for the convertible top was a metal enclosure which completely covered the canvas, but left the top ribs visible above the rear fender in a landau-iron style. Little is known of these graceful cars and few, if any, survive.

Through the various "revisions" which occurred at six-month intervals, many convenience items were offered. Philco radios, opening rear windows, sunroof openings and full instrumentation were optional accessories. Fifteen basic colors and nineteen possible color combinations of interior and exterior finishes were available. Multiple variations of accessories can be found on any of these vehicles.

SS II

At the introduction of the SS line in October 1931, a smaller four-cylinder version known as the SS II made its debut. It was based on the Standard Little Nine chassis and offered a 1006 cc engine for its first two years. Only a coupe variety was sold which was

Later SS I tourer. Note the identifying vertical bar in the grille, and the full fender indicating the later vintage of the "first revision." Michael Frostick photo.

SS I tourer (1935). This unrestored car from Harrah's Automobile Collection shows the desirable styling of the time—boot shell fenders, wire wheels and leather-covered boot. Author photo courtesy Harrah's Automobile Collection.

SS I, SS II

ENGINE

Type: 4-cylinder; 3 engine sizes available 9, 10, 12 hp
Bore x Stroke, mm: 60.25x88
Displacement: 1006 cc (1931), 1343 cc or 1608 cc (1934)
Valve Operation: side-valve
Compression Ratio: 7:1
Carburetion: SU or RAG
Bhp (Mrf): 32 to 38 @ 4000 rpm

CHASSIS & DRIVETRAIN

Transmission: Standard Motorcar Production (3-speed, 4-speed offered 1933)
Gear Ratio: 5.29:1

Frame: Standard Little Nine (Swallow modification of double drop variety)

GENERAL

Wheelbase, inches: 89.5, 104 (1934)
Track, inches: 45, 46.5 (1934)
Brakes: Bendix duo-servo
Tire Size, front and rear: 28x5.50
Wheels: Rudge-Whitworth center-lock, wire
Body Builder: Swallow Coachbuilding Company

Chassis Serial Numbers:

SS I: 135001 to 136757 (1932-33);
    247001 to 249500 (1934-36)
SS II: Nonconsecutive chassis numbers
    (1932-33); 300001 to 301250 (1934-36)

fittingly described as a "helmut-wing" style (similar to that of the Austin Seven).

In 1933, both the frame and the engine were changed. Available displacements were increased to 1343 and 1608 cc and the Little Nine chassis was replaced by Swallow's own modification of the new Standard offerings. This allowed introduction of a four-seater fixed-head coupe and a saloon. In 1934, the long, low look was enhanced by the introduction of the longer, integral fender styles which had become so popular on the SS I.

SS 90

In 1935, SS Cars, Ltd. hired William Heynes. One of his first challenges was to solve the failures of "the pretty little curving-tailed SS 90 prototype." One "boat-tailed" SS 90 roadster and twenty-three "slab-tanked" (refers to the configuration of the rear-mounted gasoline tank) roadsters were produced.

Although smaller and underpowered, as noted by the reviewers of the day, they were attractive and desirable automobiles of their era, but to be replaced by the SS 100. These attractive small roadsters are extremely rare and highly desirable today. John Rupp correctly points out that counterfeit editions of the SS 90 are known to exist and no replica of the SS 90 is currently produced. Thus, the customer is warned to research any available SS 90 and request authentication from the seller.

SS 100

In 1936, two significant changes occurred. First, the name Jaguar was added to the marque creating the name SS Jaguar. The second change involved the upgrading of the sports model which was designed "to accommodate the rigors of competitive touring on the Continent." Thus the SS 100 was born and the first of William Lyons' three masterpieces created.

The SS 100 was the first true 100 mph sports car available to the consumer, and the list of original deliveries for the cars, as published by Andrew Whyte, demonstrates immediate acceptance throughout the world. Here was a car that could rally unmodified against any comer. The subsequent four years preceding World War II would document its winning performances in speed trials, road races, endurance contests and rallies of every length and location.

The 1936-37 models, 126 in number, were equipped with the 2½ liter (2663 cc) engines but in 1938, a 3½ liter engine was introduced for the entire SS Jaguar line and some of the early models were upgraded. The low center of gravity, which was carried over from the SS I and tested in the SS 90, provided excellent handling. The brake system by Girling was retained in most Jaguar models until the advent of the V-12 models. The original tires were Dunlop sports types mounted on splined-hub wire wheels.

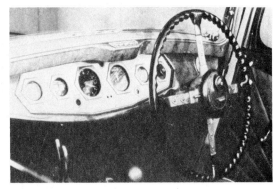

SS Cars Ltd. identification plate mounted on the driver's doorsill. Author photo.

Hexagonal trim around dashboard instruments introduced on the SS I were highly desirable at the time. Michael Frostick photo.

This stylish closed coupe, Jaguar Airline Saloon of 1935, reflects the popular Art Deco style. Note the non-standard canvas-covered spare tires in the side-mount position. The rain deflectors over the windows were standard equipment. Author photos courtesy Harrah's Automobile Collection.

Sports cars of that era offered little in creature comforts and, by today's standards, the SS 100 was no exception. For example, an unusual feature noted by *Motor* in its road test was the attachment of the top to the outside of the body shell in a "flap-proof" manner. Instrumentation was straightforward and arranged across the dashboard in the fashion of the day.

The immediate success and continuing desirability of the SS 100 lay in its magnificent proportions. Viewed from any direction, it epitomized power and few automotive designs have achieved such balance and symmetry of line. Two competitors are later designs of Lyons—the XK 120 and the XK-E. The rarity of this car—only 309 production models—has made it one of the most desirable classic sports cars regardless of marque. To own one is to have achieved one of the pinnacles of collectordom; many have settled for replicas.

The SS 100 was actively campaigned by most owners. SS Jaguar, the name of the company by then, maintained a close relationship with the SS Car Club. This encouraged reports from owners and enthusiasts and resulted in constant upgrading of the product. The restorer of the SS 100 will rapidly learn that these cars were truly "handmade" and parts interchangeability is only a dream.

SS JAGUAR SALOONS

Along with another new name for the company, SS Cars Ltd., also came a new series of sedans to the 1935 Olympia Fields fall exhibition. The classic lines, hefty performance and moderate price brought buyers flocking and the total production of the marque rose from just over 2,000 units to 5,000 units in less than two years. Contemplate the production problems and consider that the stamped-steel bodies were not introduced until 1938.

Styling advances were obvious. The spare tires were placed in the front fender. The fenders were, in turn, sculptured to accommodate this intrusion but retained the graceful curve first seen in the SS I, expanded in the SS 90 and culminated in the SS 100. This look became the most desired style in the last years before the war. It certainly echoed the larger, more expensive styling seen in the custom bodies built in the US and in England. So desirable was the styling that it remained essentially intact until 1948 with only minor changes in contour dictated by the switch to pressed-steel bodies in 1938. Heaters and piston dampers in both engines were added to all models in 1940. Optional radios were discontinued in late 1939 but restored after the end of the war.

The SS saloon was produced with three engine selections: a 1½ liter (1776 cc), a 2½ liter (2663 cc) and a 3½ liter (3485 cc). When the saloon was introduced in 1935, the former two engines

An Airline Saloon with optional features: full fender skirts, full covered side mounts and quad-mounted driving lights. Author collection.

An SS I tourer of later vintage. Michael Frostick, Andrew Whyte photo.

An early SS II. Note cycle-style fenders and absence of the three-quarter window. Author collection.

were available and the latter engine was added in 1938. The smaller engine became immensely popular, in spite of its relatively weak performance, because of its attractive price.

Inside, such standard features as well-laid-out Smith instrumentation in a French walnut dashboard, Vaumol leather hides on the doors as well as the seats, and a sliding roof (sunroof) no doubt added to the immediate success. Standard features included a complete tool set arranged in a padded case mounted in the trunk lid and a mechanism to open the windshield. Lest the reader lose perspective, these features, which seem commonplace today, were optional features on the most expensive custom-bodied automobiles of the era. William Lyons offered all of them with essentially only a choice of engine sizes, at a price from 285 to 395 pounds Sterling.

In 1937, wind vents and mechanically driven windshield wipers were fitted. The walnut dashboard was rearranged to provide a glove compartment (cubbyhole) for each side. Armrests and pockets in the doors were added for rear seat passenger convenience. The tool kit at the back lid was illuminated and hinged outward for convenience.

In 1938, the emminently successful body was reworked with careful attention to maintain the style. New, pressed-steel bodies were fitted on a new, X-braced cross-frame to provide greater width and interior room. The famous P-100 headlamps were fitted to the 1938 3½ liter saloons. Perhaps the most recognizable feature, which was changed in the 1938 models, was the movement of the spare tire from the left front fender-mount position to a separate compartment beneath the trunk. Turn signals, mounted in the crown of the front fenders, were added at this time and became a Jaguar styling feature that would persist until the end of the XK 150 model production.

In 1938, a drop-head coupe was added to the line. The successful design of the SS sedans (saloons) was strengthened to accommodate this stylish two-door convertible with its landau irons. It was also offered with all options and three engine choices. Although most SS cars were delivered with the eighteen-inch Rutledge wheels, Michael Frostick has a photograph in his book, *The Jaguar Tradition*, of Ace discs fitted, giving the effect of solid wheels.

Revisions for the 1939 models were minimal, reflecting mostly refinements to the existing mechanical systems.

With the onset of World War II, production dropped from 5,378 units in 1939 to 899 units in 1940 and then ceased as all attention was turned to the support of the war effort. In this regard the factory at Foleshill turned itself to the production and repair of aircraft parts especially for Spitfire fighter planes, Mosquito light bombers and Sterling heavy bombers.

Dashboard of SS II and view of interior restored to original specifications. Author photo.

SS II drop-head convertible. Although shorter, the lines are well proportioned and pleasing even with the top up. Author photo.

SS 90 shown in three-quarter front view. Author collection.

Note the "buried" spare tire placement of this SS 90. Author collection.

SS 90

ENGINE
Type: in-line 6-cylinder
Bore x Stroke, mm: 73x106
Displacement: 2663 cc
Valve Operation: side-valve
Compression Ratio: 7:1
Carburetion: twin RAG
Bhp (Mrf): 20

CHASSIS & DRIVETRAIN
Transmission: 4-speed synchromesh in top
 3 gears
Rear Suspension: semielliptical springs

Gear Ratio: 4.28:1, 3.75:1 (optional for
 speed trials)
Front Suspension: semielliptical spring
Frame: box (lengthened from the SS I)

GENERAL
Wheelbase, inches: 104
Track, inches: 54
Brakes: Bendix duo-servo
Tire Size, front and rear: 5.25(5.50)x18
Wheels: 18-inch Rudge-Whitworth
Body Builder: SS Cars Ltd.

Chassis Serial Numbers:
248436 to 249498

View from the cockpit of the SS 100. Note the efficient dashboard design created for the two-man rallying team. The view over the hood emphasizes the excitement of driving this car. Note the small racing windshield mounted in front of the driver. Author photo courtesy Harrah's Automobile Collection.

SS 100 from Harrah's Automobile Collection. This classic version of the "sports car" of the thirties is easily recognized by the headlights with the stone guards. The center-mounted driving light was an optional feature. Compare the styling of this two-seater with the four-seater SS I in the background. Author photo courtesy Harrah's Automobile Collection.

Note the canvas-covered, single rear-mounted spare tire, the balanced boat-shell fenders, the dashboard style and the slab gas tank. All are unique styling features of the SS 100. Author photo courtesy Harrah's Automobile Collection.

SS 100

ENGINE
Type: in-line 6-cylinder
Bore x Stroke, mm: 73x106, 82x110
Displacement: 2663 cc (2½L), 3485 cc (3½L)
Valve Operation: overhead, pushrod,
   spring-mounted
Compression Ratio: 7:1 (2½L), 7.2:1 (3½L)
Carburetion: twin SU
Bhp (Mrf): 104 (3½L)

CHASSIS & DRIVETRAIN
Transmission: 4 speeds forward and reverse
   (central control)
Rear Suspension: semielliptical spring
Gear Ratio: 4.0, 5.5, 8.45, 13.6:1

Front Suspension: semielliptical spring
Frame: box section (stiffened)

GENERAL
Wheelbase, inches: 104
Track, front, inches: 63
      rear, inches: 63
Brakes: Girling drum
Tire Size, front and rear: 5.25x18
Wheels: center knock-off, wire
Body Builder: SS Cars Ltd.
Chassis Serial Numbers:
18001 to 18126 2½L (1936-37)
49001 to 49065 2½L (1938-40)
39001 to 39118 3½L (1938-40)

SWALLOW TO JAGUAR 1922-72

The SS 100 of Holly Hollenbeck as shown on the poster issued to commemorate the fiftieth anniversary of Jaguar Cars in 1972. Another SS 100 is seen at speed in the background. Jaguar Cars, Inc., author collection.

The early SS Jaguar saloon (1936), identified by its side mount and truncated appearance. Note the bumper-mounted horns which were carried over from the SS I cars. Michael Frostick photo.

A 1938 SS Jaguar saloon. This was the first of the all-steel bodies and is identifiable by the absence of the side mount. Michael Frostick photo.

SS SALOON

ENGINE

Type: in-line 6-cylinder overhead valve (2½, 3½L), standard side-valve engine (1½L)

Displacement: 1608 cc (1½L) or 1776 cc (later); 2663 cc (2½L) (ohv engine 1938); 3485 cc (3½L)

Valve Operation: pushrod

Compression Ratio: 7:1 (2½L), 7.2:1 (3½L)

Carburetion: twin SU

Bhp (Mrf): 104 (3½L)

CHASSIS & DRIVETRAIN

Transmission: 4-speeds forward and reverse (central control)

Rear Suspension: semielliptical spring

Gear Ratio: 4.0, 5.5, 8.45, 13.6:1

Front Suspension: semielliptical spring

Frame: wood box, changed to X-braced in 1938 with the adaptation of pressed-steel bodies

GENERAL

Wheelbase, inches: 108 (1½L), 119 (2½, 3½L), 120 (steel body)

Track, front, inches: 48 (1½L), 54 (2½, 3½L) rear, inches: 48 (1½L), 54 (2½, 3½L)

Brakes: Giching d

Tire Size, front and rear: 5.25x18

Wheels: 18-inch center, knock-off wire

Body Builder: SS Cars Ltd.

Chassis Serial Numbers:

10001 to 13445 2½L Saloon (1936-37)
19001 to 19105 2½L Tourer (1936-37)
20001 to 22250 1½L Saloon (1936-37)
30001 to 31003 3½L Saloon (1938-39)
36001 to 36238 3½L DHC (1938-39)
40001 to 41445 2½L Saloon (1938-39)
46001 to 46273 2½L DHC (1938-39)
50001 to 53754 1½L Saloon (1938-39)
56001 to 56660 1½L DHC (1938-39)
70001 to 70668 1½L Saloon/DHC (1940)
80001 to 80135 2½L Saloon/DHC (1940)
90001 to 90068 3½L Saloon/DHC (1940)

Original lines of this 1938 SS Jaguar saloon have been modified by the fender-mounted rearview mirrors and the change in the position of the driving lights. Author photo.

A 1938 SS Jaguar drop-head coupe. It is very similar to the 1946 Jaguar drop-head. Author photo.

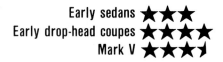

Early sedans ★★★
Early drop-head coupes ★★★★
Mark V ★★★⌁

When the war effort finally wound down, the first Jaguar cars became available by October 1945. Sharp observation was needed to note the few changes instituted. The rear marque identification was a monogram J, indicative of the new company name—Jaguar Cars Ltd.—and the famous hexagon rim was missing. The SS name had been quietly laid to rest for obvious reasons. The major manufacturing advance for the company was the acquisition of the machinery to manufacture six-cylinder engines from Standard Car Company Ltd.

The first models offered by Jaguar Cars Ltd. were the saloons with the familiar 1½, 2½ and 3½ liter engines. Most changes were purely mechanical—updated axle and brake design. Modifications to the heating system were added and were reflected in a new dashboard style with the control levers located on the lower border of the central section. This feature and the winged marque identification on the grille border are the only easily identifiable differences between the early postwar and the late prewar saloons.

The drop-head coupe was added in 1947; significantly, left-hand-drive options were added for the first time to accommodate the increased demand of the American market. According to Jack Rabell, forty percent drop-head coupes and 640 saloons, of a production run totalling 12,042 vehicles, were equipped with left-hand drive. Minor mechanical improvements were added and by the middle of 1949, when the Mark V was introduced, the production totals for the thirty-two-month period had risen to 11,952 units which included 104 2½ liter drop-head coupes and 560 3½ liter drop-head coupes.

THE MARK V

In late 1948, the first true postwar Jaguar was introduced. Although the English automotive press, who were eagerly awaiting the rumored new models, provided extensive commentary, Andrew Whyte perhaps analyzed the changes best as "subtle."

A 1946-47 drop-head coupe is distinguished by its uncluttered features when compared to its newer counterparts. Author photo.

THE POSTWAR SALOON/DROP-HEAD

ENGINE

Type: in-line 4-cylinder pushrod (1½L), in-line 6-cylinder ohv (2½, 3½L)

Bore x Stroke, mm: 73x106 (1½L, 4cyl), 73x 106 (2½L, 6cyl), 82x110 (3½L)

Displacement: 1776 cc, 2663 cc, 3485 cc

Valve Operation: pushrod

Compression Ratio: 7.5:1 (1½L), 7.6:1 (2½L), 7.2:1 (3½L)

Carburetion: twin SU (single in 1½L)

Bhp (Mrf): 65 (1½L), 102 (2½L), 125 (3½L)

CHASSIS & DRIVETRAIN

Transmission: 4 speeds forward and reverse, central control

Rear Suspension: semielliptical spring

Gear Ratio: 4.87, 7.08, 11.84, 19.21:1 (1½L); 4.55, 6.12, 8.82, 15.36:1 (2½L); 4.27, 5.14, 8.28, 14.41:1 (3½L)

Front Suspension: semielliptical spring

Frame: X-braced steel

GENERAL

Wheelbase, inches: 112½ (1½L), (steel body 2½L, 3½L)

Track, front, inches: 52 (1½L), 54 (2½, 3½L) rear, inches: 55 (1½L), 56 (2½, 3½L)

Brakes: Girling rod-operated

Tire Size, front and rear: 5.25x18 (1½L); 5.50x 18 (2½, 3½L)

Wheels: 18-inch center, knock-off wire

Body Builder: Jaguar Cars Ltd.

Chassis Serial Numbers: (Note—Six-digit numbers in all postwar series)

1½L Saloon/DHC 410000 on (1946-48)

2½L Saloon (RHD) 510000 on (1946-48)

2½L DHC (RHD) 517000 on (1947-48)

2½L Saloon (LHD) 530000 on (1947-48)

2½L DHC (LHD) 537000 on (1947-48)

3½L Saloon (RHD) 610000 on (1946-48)

3½L DHC (RHD) 617000 on (1947-48)

3½L Saloon (LHD) 630000 on (1947-48)

3½L DHC (LHD) 637000 on (1947-48)

The model was offered in the two familiar body styles: the saloon and the drop-head. The styling theme was modernized with the flaring of the headlights into the front fenders and enlarging the grille dimensions. Both seemed to balance the heavy appearance of the full fender skirts. The wheel rims were reduced from the traditional eighteen inches to a substantial sixteen-inch variety, which blended with the overall tone of solidarity. Compensating for the bulky appearance, however, the raked windshield lent a racy attitude.

The biggest mechanical advance of the model was the introduction of the independent front suspension. The major changes included the dropping production of the popular 1½ liter engines and the severance of connections with Standard Car. But a number of innovative features distinguished this series. The trunk was now illuminated by a manually controlled switch which worked when the headlamps or parking lamps were turned on. Push-button door locks and flatter floors were industry-leading features.

Both sedan (saloon) and drop-head models of the Mark V were produced from 1949 through 1951. A total of 10,466 units was delivered. By 1950, the entire factory production was devoted to increasing the unit production totals of the XK 120 and the improvements on the Mark V were minimal. Refinements included improving the technique for removing and replacing the rear-wheel fender skirts and the hood latches. Undoubtedly, a position change of the front seat was in response to owner comments. The drop-head coupe received a heavier centerpost (removable) and a less-complicated mechanism to place the soft top in any of its three positions.

One distinguishing feature of the 1950 model run was the elevation of the front bumpers and placement of air vents in the lower fender surfaces. This attempted to solve the tendency of the Girling brakes to fade when overheated.

The potential Jaguar buyer should be made aware of the so-called Mark IV. This term is frequently used to designate the saloons and coupe models produced from 1945-46 through 1949, prior to the introduction of the Mark V. There has never been such a factory designation and any Jaguar advertised as such must be examined carefully and then researched. Similarly, there has never been a Mark VI. This designation was used by Bentley for its first postwar model and avoided by Jaguar to prevent confusion.

Close-up of the new radiator emblem adopted after World War II when the SS classification was dropped. Author collection.

Rear three-quarter view emphasizing the clean lines of the post-war car. Note also the left-hand drive which was characteristic of this model. This model is occasionally called the Mark IV but the term is unofficial. Author photo.

The 1948 Mark V drop-head coupe. Note the partially enclosed headlights, the solid wheels and the fender skirts which distinguish this postwar model. Author photo.

THE MARK V

ENGINE
Type: in-line 6-cylinder
Bore x Stroke, mm: 73x106 (2½L), 82x110 (3½L)
Displacement: 2663 cc (2½L), 3485 cc (3½L)
Valve Operation: pushrod
Compression Ratio: 7.2:1 (2½L), 6.75:1 (3½L)
Carburetion: twin SU
Bhp (Mrf): 102, 125

CHASSIS & DRIVETRAIN
Transmission: 4-speed (synchromesh except 2nd to 1st gear)
Rear Suspension: semielliptical
Gear Ratio: 4.55, 6.21, 9.01, 15.35:1 (2½L); 4.3, 5.87, 8.52, 14.8:1 (3½L)
Front Suspension: independent with torsion bar

Frame: X-member steel

GENERAL
Wheelbase, inches: 120
Track, front, inches: 56.5
    rear, inches: 57.5
Brakes: Girling 2LS hydraulic
Tire Size, front and rear: 6.70x16
Wheels: pressed-steel hubs
Body Builder: Jaguar Cars Ltd.

Chassis Serial Numbers:
Mark V (1949-51) 2.5L Saloon (LHD) 527001 on
2.5L DHC (LHD) 547001 on
3.5L Saloon (LHD) 627001 on
3.5L DHC (LHD) 647001 on
2.5L Saloon (RHD) 520001 on
2.5L DHC (RHD) 540001 on
3.5L Saloon (RHD) 620001 on
3.5L DHC (RHD) 640001 on

Mark V trunk space. Note very finished appearance. Complete tool kit is contained in trunk lid compartment. Author photo.

This Mark V sedan has nonstandard white sidewall tires and leaping Jaguar hood ornament. These models achieved marked success in touring car competition. *E-Jag* photo.

The first postwar motorcar show held in England began on October 27, 1948, and the motoring public was totally unprepared for the sleek bronze roadster in the Jaguar booth. With the introduction of the XK 120, William Lyons set a new style and pace of sports car production.

Two events were celebrated that evening: the major styling advance of the XK 120 series and, perhaps even more important, the debut of the double overhead camshaft (dohc) engine, which has been the mainstay of Jaguar cars for over three decades. This engine, which would be common to all Jaguar cars until the advent of the V-12 in 1971, underwent several factory modifications during the XK 120 run and additional powerplant options were available to those who read the fine print. The obvious implication for the buyer of a used Jaguar is to have proper identification of the engine.

The original engine was a 3.4 liter (3442 cc) block equipped with a chain-driven double overhead camshaft. In 1951, a Special Equipment package was offered by Jaguar to satisfy the competitive consumers. This included newly designed pistons, which raised the standard 7:1 compression ratio to 8:1. Engines so equipped had the engine serial number prefaced by a 7 or an 8. Also included in this equipment package were the complementary ignition and carburetion package and a camshaft with a 3/8-inch lift. A lighter flywheel and stiffer suspension items (torsion bars and rear springs) completed the mechanical part of the package. With the introduction of the racing C-type in 1953, a competition head became available and found its way into some XK 120's. This raised the compression ratio to 9:1. It is easily identified by the distinctive red paint ("red head"). If the original brushed aluminum head covers are present, they are cast with a hexagonal C emblem. Some units with this head installed are advertised as XK 120C or XKC but no official designation was endorsed by the factory.

Another head noted in production was the B-type, which is identified by its blue color. A later variation that found its way

An XK 120 roadster of early vintage equipped with steel wheels and rear fender skirts. This unrestored, but well kept, example (owned by Thomas Lewis) has had the parking lights removed from the crest of the fenders. Author photo.

Rear view of restored XK 120 roadster. Note bumper guards— especially their size and location. Author photo.

onto some dohc engines was the gold head of the D-type engine. As the engine block was common, head switching was frequent and many combinations are seen.

The initial model of the XK 120 was the classic roadster. In 1951, a fixed-head coupe (FHC) was introduced to satisfy those who wanted better protection from the weather. The drop-head coupe (DHC; convertible, in American terms) was introduced in April 1953.

The Special Equipment group available after 1951 included wire wheels and dual exhaust for an extra $395. In the United States, cars so equipped were more commonly referred to as modified and designated with a suffix M (such as XK 120M). The wire wheels originally supplied in the M package were painted to match the exterior color of the car but, late in the XK 120 model run, factory-supplied chrome wire wheels became available. If the car was delivered with wire wheels instead of the standard pressed-steel wheels, the rear wheel covers were left off. A detachable metal strip, painted to match the body, was used to finish the fender-well edge.

The original nine colors offered to the buyer in 1949 were expanded to forty-one by late 1952. Although any car may have nonoriginal paint, a premium price may be sought for original paint and interiors.

The graceful styling and innovative mechanics make the XK 120 one of the most desirable Jaguar models to obtain. Prices for these cars have risen steadily since the late sixties and have maintained their levels. The fixed-head and the drop-head are scarcer but the classic simplicity of the roadster makes it a most desirable Jaguar, only surpassed by the SS 100.

THE ROADSTER

The roadster was introduced in October 1949 and the demand was instantaneous. It was a true roadster with a fully detachable top which stored in the trunk. Side curtains, with Plexiglas windows in them, were mounted to the doors to complete the weather protection.

Production began at the rate of twelve units a month and slowly increased to a total production run of 7,631 units. The first 240 XK 120 units delivered were equipped with an aluminum alloy body. A buyer is advised that while these models are rarer and definitely more desirable, the restoration will be more difficult due to the "by-hand" manufacturing techniques employed. In early 1950, stamped-steel bodies were introduced and parts interchangeability became feasible.

Few special options were available for the roadster. One notable exception was the aeroscreens which graced the first roadsters seeking the highly publicized speed records. After 132.6 mph had been clocked at Jabbeke, Belgium, the remaining cars

Another example of the classic. This is a later model with the M modifications. Different car, but same model. Author photos.

produced that year (1950) were outfitted with a dash plaque emblematic of the event. That same record-setting car possessed an undershield. According to author Paul Skilleter, only one still exists and it is unmounted.

Two styling improvements made during the model run, which will not be apparent to the uninitiated, are changes to the turn signals on the front fenders and the rearview mirror style. In the early models, the turn signal indicator covers were chrome plated and externally mounted. With the advent of the fixed-head coupe in 1951, all models had the fitting welded into the fender and painted to match. The early models had short-necked inside rearview mirror mounts while the later models were longer.

THE FIXED-HEAD COUPE (FHC)

March 1951 saw the addition of a closed, fixed-head coupe to the Jaguar line. The FHC, as it was called, bore distinct styling heritage to the saloons while preserving the gracefully flowing lines which had made the XK 120 series so immensely popular.

The engine and drivetrain were similar throughout the line and no distinct modifications were employed on the FHC. The addition of self-adjusting brakes for all models occurred in 1952 after being proven on the C-type.

The interior appointments of the fixed-head were pleasantly different. The dashboard and all trim plates were of burled walnut veneer. The amenities of the touring car were introduced —such as roll-up windows, air vents, glove compartments, map containers in the door, sun visors, interior lights and foot-well vents. (The latter were introduced to all models to improve ventilation in the passenger compartment.) A heater, which had been optional on the roadster without provision for a defogger (defroster), became standard on both models when the fixed-head was introduced.

Style variations, which were basically improvements, also accompanied the introduction of the fixed-head coupe and were integrated into the roadster. These included the utilization of the same color leather for the entire seat cover differing from the early roadsters where one darker color surrounded a lighter one.

No space was available behind the seat of the XK 120 fixed-head or drop-head coupe. The finish panels hinged forward to allow access to the twin 6-volt batteries, mounted side by side, behind the seats.

THE DROP-HEAD COUPE (DHC)

The obvious expression of the SS and SS Jaguar heritage made its debut in 1953—the drop-head coupe. It is further suggested that the XK 120 drop-head coupe was an experiment conducted in response to the American dealers who wanted improved weather protection and conveniences for their customers while main-

XK 120 roadster dashboard. Note standard pointed horn button and stock steering wheel. Gear shift knob is nonstandard. Author photo.

XK 120M fixed-head coupe sporting wire wheels. This English model has right-hand drive and unsealed headlights. Author collection.

taining the open car. After all, the American dealers were competing with the "all-American dream machines" of the fifties. Although some element of logic exists in the latter theory, the tradition of drop-head coupes stretching back to the SS I and SS II models is hard to deny. I feel it should be considered a natural evolution. In any event, my experience in attempting to match finish parts for my DHC suggests strongly that much of the body fit was individual. One wonders whether the immense popularity of this model was anticipated and production techniques were only explored in the small production run of the XK 120 drop-head coupe (1,769 units).

Combining the weather protection of the fixed-head and the open feeling of the roadster was a natural, and the beautifully tailored tops maintained the lines accurately. But, if one of these highly desirable and rare models is purchased for restoration, the top will need to be handmade.

Few mechanical variations occurred during the short model run of this car. The Salisbury rear axle was standard on this car. However, the C-type head and its accessory carburetors were available and some cars were fitted with them.

XK 120

ENGINE
Type: dohc in-line 6-cylinder
Bore x Stroke, mm: 83x106
Displacement: 3442 cc (3.4L)
Valve Operation: overhead camshaft
Compression Ratio: 7:1, 8:1 (optional), 9:1 in C-head
Carburetion: twin SU
Bhp (Mrf): 160, 180, (Sp. Eq. or M)
CHASSIS & DRIVETRAIN
Transmission: 4-speed synchromesh (except first)
Rear Suspension: semielliptical
Gear Ratio: 3.64, 4.98, 7.22, 12.29:1; Salisbury
Front Suspension: independent
Frame: reinforced cross-member steel

GENERAL
Wheelbase, inches: 102
Track, front, inches: 51
    rear, inches: 51
Brakes: Lockheed 2LS hydraulic
Tire Size, front and rear: 6.00x16
Wheels: pressed-steel; wire available in Special Equipment package
Body Builder: Jaguar Cars Ltd.
Chassis Serial Numbers:
Roadster (RHD) 660001 on
(LHD) 670001 on
Fixed-Head Coupe (RHD) 669001 on
(LHD) 679001 on
Drop-Head Coupe (RHD) 667001 on
(LHD) 677001 on
S prefix to any number indicates Special Equipment model

The engine compartment of a restored XK 120 roadster with the C-type head. (The red color of the cylinder head is not easily seen.) Note the location of the identification plaque on the fire-wall, as this is common to all models of XK 120. Author photo.

XK 120 fixed-head coupe in standard delivery trim—steel wheels and fender skirts. Michael Frostick photo.

Dashboard from XK 120 drop-head. Burled veneer wood and dash-board arrangement was the same for the fixed-head coupe; but compare it with roadster dash. Note automatic transmission shift lever (rare) and nonstandard radio, horn button and steering wheel. Author photo.

XK 120M drop-head coupe with top down and without the top cover in place—owned by John R. McGill. This photo illustrates the point that the classic lines were not disturbed by the addition of the Americanized convertible top. Author photo.

This immaculate XK 120M (modified) roadster sports wire wheels and no fender skirts. Outfitted for racing, the windshield has been removed and replaced with individual windscreens. The bumpers have been removed to reduce weight. Author photo.

Another XK 120M drop-head coupe shown to illustrate an owner's choice of modifications—oversized tires, fog lights (standard option) and non-standard radio antenna. Author photo.

Roadster ★★★★↙
Other models ★★★★

The six model-run years of the XK 120 series suggested refinements for the car. The design certainly was pleasing but extra room, standard wire wheels and more power were constant requests of the consumer (especially in America). Thus, in response, October 1954 saw the introduction of the XK 140 with major changes in appearance and engineering.

Externally, the classic lines were retained but were protected by sturdier bumpers specifically designed from the Mark VII sedan molds to give better protection, both front and rear, on American streets. The fragile XK 120 grille, which tended to lose "teeth" at the slightest insult, was replaced by a heavier unit with fewer teeth but more strength. The front fenders now sported low-mounted, round turn signal indicators in addition to the parking lights located on the crest. Special Equipment models were easily identified by the presence of Lucas FT 576 fog lamps mounted on the horizontal surface of the front bumper (splash) pan.

From the rear, the basic lines remained but the finish features were completely restyled. The trunk lid now carried a vertical center chrome line, drawing attention to the medallion in the middle, which proclaimed the Le Mans wins of the marque. The license plate mount now occupied the center of the bumper line and took the license plate illuminator and back-up light down with it. The rear bumper wrapped around the fenders in a protective fashion and sported vertical bumper guards. The exhaust pipe exited to the left side on the standard issue but the dual exhaust system delivered with the C head was identified by the placement of one pipe beneath each bumper guard.

Inside, the front seat and the dashboard remained the same as in the XK 120 for each model. The most noticeable difference was the added room in the front seat area afforded by the movement of the engine block forward on the chassis.

Although the external appearance of the XK 140 was significantly altered (a few say improved), the major changes were mechanical. The most important change was the reposition-

The most common model of the XK 140, usually found in America —the drop-head coupe. This example is owned by Micheal Mahoney. Author photo.

ing of the engine three inches forward on the chassis. This not only afforded additional passenger room, it also provided space for the battery in the front fender well, thus freeing the area behind the seats for a "jump seat" and/or additional storage, depending on the model. This produced a significant change in the road handling by shifting the balance of car weight to the front axle. This handling change gave greater straight-line stability but tended to produce some understeer on cornering. The second major improvement was the fitting of Alford and Alder rack-and-pinion steering.

The standard XK 140 was powered by the 190 bhp in-line double overhead cam six-cylinder engine. However, a Special Equipment version could be obtained which included the C (red) head developed for the C-type Le Mans racer. This package carried with it a dual exhaust system (somewhat reworked and rerouted from the XK 120), wire wheels and fog lights. Thus it is easy to identify the Special Equipment models of this series. Frequently these are suffixed "M" (for modified) as in the XK 120 series.

The major problem with the XK 140 series, as a whole, was the braking system. The added weight and the added power produced a tendency to fade, especially with heat buildup. Several solutions were tried but the real answer awaited the disc brakes introduced on the XK 150 model. The wheel sizes and arrangements were essentially the same, however.

XK 140 series hubcaps for the pressed-steel wheels could be easily recognized, as they were all chrome rather than chrome and matching body-color paint as on the XK 120.

THE ROADSTER

The changes mentioned were more or less common to all three models. The roadster, however, required additional modification of the body to accommodate the additional three inches of interior space gained by the relocation of the engine. The rear body sheetmetal was extended forward and the new enclosed space behind the seats was added to the storage compartment. A convenience shelf for storage of the sidescreens was also added. The back wall of this compartment folded down allowing direct access to the trunk.

The interior roadster trim remained similar to that of the XK 120 except that the horn plate was flattened for driver safety. The windshield was still removable and all competition options were available.

The roadster in its left-hand-drive (LHD or export) version is the most common model of the entire production run. However, the rarest of the XK 140's is the right-hand-drive (RHD) roadster—only seventy-three units were built.

Note split, heavier rear bumper which wraps around the rear fenders for additional protection. Author photo.

THE FIXED-HEAD COUPE (FHC)

Small but major changes were made in the size and shape of the greenhouse of the XK 140 FHC. Each dimension was increased by raising the top line, moving the windshield forward and the rear window backward. This increased the interior room significantly, increased the "glass space" and gave the passenger a better spatial arrangement. Lengthening the top also allowed the doors to be widened making entrance and exit easier.

The rear compartment now possessed enough room to allow two "jump seats" to be installed. Early models are said to have been delivered with separate high-back seats but most XK 140's seen today have the short version. This allowed easy access to the rear wall, which was hinged similar to the roadster.

THE DROP-HEAD COUPE (DHC)

The drop-head coupe enjoyed all the benefits of the other models —improved handling, rear jump seats, rack-and-pinion steering, to mention a few. It, along with the fixed-head coupe, began a definite trend away from the totally sports- or competition-oriented automobile concept and toward the theme of a posh touring car built for high-speed travel. Obviously, the XK 140, and the XK 150 to follow, were successful in this goal in the mid-fifties and remain so today.

XK 140

ENGINE

Type: dohc in-line 6-cylinder
Bore x Stroke, mm: 83x106
Displacement: 3442 cc
Valve Operation: cam-operated
Compression Ratio: 8:1, 9:1 (C-head, M)
Carburetion: twin SU
Bhp (Mrf): 190, 210 (C-head)

CHASSIS & DRIVETRAIN

Transmission: 4-speed synchromesh (except first); late DHC and FHC hand automatic Borg-Warner transmission options
Rear Suspension: semielliptical spring
Gear Ratio: 3.54, 4.83, 7.01, 11.95:1
Front Suspension: independent
Frame: X-braced steel

GENERAL

Wheelbase, inches: 102

Track, front and rear, inches: 51.5
Brakes: Lockheed 2LS hydraulic
Tire Size, front and rear: 16-inch
Wheels: wire standard, pressed-steel available
Body Builder: Jaguar Cars Ltd.

Chassis Serial Numbers:

Roadster (RHD) 800001 on (1954-57)
    (LHD) 810001 on (1954-57)
Fixed-head coupe (RHD) 804001 on (1954-57)
    (LHD) 814001 on (1954-57)
Drop-head coupe (RHD) 807001 on (1954-57)
    (LHD) 817001 on (1954-57)
S prefix to any number indicates Special Equipment model with C-type head
A prefix to any model indicates Special Equipment model with standard head
DN suffix indicates overdrive addition

From the XK 140 series, a drop-head coupe (light color) and a rarer roadster. Note the parking lights placed low in the fenders and the variations in the license plate mounts. The purchaser chose between the wire wheels and the pressed-steel wheels, as both were standard. Driving lights (mounted on the bumper pan) were an optional accessory. Author photo.

Engine compartment of XK 140 drop-head. Note location of identification plate on horizontal section of firewall (top center of photograph). Author photo.

The XK 140 fixed-head coupe. Note the changes in the roof line and window configuration from the XK 120 series. Michael Frostick photo.

Interior of the XK 140 roadster. Note the slanted instrument panel and the flattened horn button. The gear shift knob shown is stock. Author photo.

The XK 140 roadster. Note the rear fender skirts, standard with pressed-steel wheels. Compare the roof lines and fender openings of the roadster with the fixed-head coupe in the background. Author photo.

CHAPTER 5
THE XK 150
1959-1961

During the production years of the XK 140, engineering advances responded to consumer demands, as Jaguars were driven daily in the United Kingdom and the United States and raced competitively on several continents. The introduction of the XK 150 series incorporated new advances to solve existing problems and keep the series contemporary.

The styling advances were immediately apparent and, visually, were a logical progression from the earlier models but also responsive to the demands of the engineers. The same frame existed but the body was wider, permitting increased interior space. The exterior styling, however, became bulkier and some of the "Lyons line" effect was lost as the hip line was straightened. The larger grille, now more square than oval, permitted better airflow to the engine compartment, but returned to a sturdier version of the thin vertical bars of the XK 120. The windshield was a "wraparound" one-piece version reflecting the styling trends common in the US. The appearance of the front bumper was softened by the addition of a gentle dip in the center segment. The rear bumper was extended completely across the rear (in contrast to the XK 140), providing additional stability and design coordination. Additional chrome trim about the exterior edges was found. The rear license-plate-mount molding (surround) for the 1960 models had trim continuous with the center chrome strip on the trunk while earlier models did not. Almost the entire production run of the XK 150 was equipped with wire wheels. Factory models equipped with disc wheels and rear wheel covers are extremely rare. Most of the other features were applicable to both of the original models: the fixed-head and the drop-head coupes. Otherwise, dashboard layout, seating arrangement and driver conveniences were similar to the XK 140 series. The concerns for inadequate interior ventilation and design of the gearshift and overdrive levers still surfaced in critical reviews. Although these criticisms had been voiced before, they were now appropriate—and Jaguar lagged behind the competitive marques of the late fifties.

The XK 150 drop-head coupe (top) shows the wraparound wind-shield which distinguishes this series. The roadster (bottom), in-troduced later in the model run, emphasized the new "hip" line. Paul Skilleter photos.

Engineering advances were the hallmark of the XK 150 model run. The introduction of Dunlop disc brakes reflected the systems used on the C-type and D-type racing cars. Disc brakes had been available on several other English cars before they were utilized on the Jaguar, but when introduced, included a unique servo mechanism to assist the driver in increasing intake manifold pressure by decreasing the needed foot pressure in the initial phases of braking. The hand brake also was given a separate caliper on the rear disc but due to its novelty it was often not adjusted properly.

The 3.4 liter engine was by now tried and true, having had successful models of sports cars, racing cars and sedans demonstrate its power and durability. The standard B-type head evolved from the C-type head of XK 120 and C-type fame. It changed the design and diameter of the intake ports with the resulting effect of lowering the engine revolutions needed for maximum power. The B-type head was recognized by the letter B cast into the burnished aluminum camshaft and valve-cover housing on the passenger side. Also, this engine could be identified by a separate water hose running along the top of the intake manifold. Beneath the engine, a metal "sump-guard" was fitted to some of the export models. The drive shaft and transmission ratios were essentially the same as those found on the XK 140.

Factory extras were few on the XK 150. The choice of transmissions—standard, standard with overdrive, or automatic —and the installation of a Smith radio were the only concerns of the purchaser. If wire wheels were fitted, "rimbellishers" were available to offer a more finished appearance to the rear wheel openings. Special seating options, available on the Mark VIII sedans, were manufactured by Reutter for the XK 150 by special request. These seats offered full adjustability and greater comfort, but were finished in the same materials and style.

During the XK 150 model run (May 1957 through March 1961), a significant engine modification became available, the S engine which featured changes in the head and intake manifold design. Intake port design had long interested Harry Weslake, Jaguar's chief engineer. By "straightening" the ports and altering the diameters, the compression ratio could be increased to 9:1. The better flow of the fuel mixture allowed the fitting of three SU carburetors to a newly designed intake manifold. Additional changes in the design and structure of the bearings, clutch and flywheel were made in anticipation of the additional torque and wear.

Late in the model run, the 3.8 liter engine was introduced. It had been developed and pioneered in the Mark IX sedan the previous year. After its success was established, it was made available for the XK 150 models. However, it generated confusion

XK 150 roadster emphasizing the styling changes most evident in the grille and the notched front bumper. Author photo.

for the buyer—then and now—as four combinations of engine and head were available and these could be specified to have one of three compression ratios, for a dazzling total of twelve variations!

The identification-plate engine serial number defined the engine as delivered from the factory. A V indicated the 3.4 liter engine with a B-type head. The VA designation indicated a 3.8 liter engine. The addition of S (VS or VAS, for example) indicated that an S-type head had been fitted in place of the B-type. Externally, the S-type models can be identified by an S placed on the passenger door beneath the quarter-window. Through the years many owners have modified their engines to achieve more power. The potential XK 150 buyer is encouraged to examine the engine/model combination carefully.

The XK 150 was initially offered in the fixed-head and drop-head varieties. However, later in the model run, a roadster was introduced.

THE FIXED-HEAD COUPE (FHC)

The introduction of the XK 150 series in October 1957, at the annual Earl's Court Show, presented only two models: the fixed-head coupe (FHC) and the drop-head coupe (DHC). Except for those changes already mentioned, this fixed-head coupe differed little from the XK 140 FHC, with the addition of some modest increases in interior space. The interior appointments still reflected comfort with leather and piping but armrests and door pulls were now standard fit. A rolled, padded dashboard was new.

THE DROP-HEAD COUPE (DHC)

As with the fixed-head coupe, there were few changes inside the drop-head coupe (convertible). Classic owners decried the loss of the burled walnut dashboard and interior trim. However, most owners appreciated the extra room afforded by the slightly wider body and thinner doors.

THE ROADSTER

In May of 1958, the XK 150 line was completed with the addition of the open roadster. The wider body lent an overall lower appearance and it is my opinion that the roadster is one of the most pleasing Jaguar designs. Addition of exterior door handles made it the first postwar roadster so equipped.

The exterior design shared styling features with the DHC and FHC. Most XK 150 roadsters were exported and, therefore, possessed left-hand drive (LHD). So a right-hand-drive (RHD) roadster is a very desirable car; and one with the S engine installed would be a real gem.

The same XK 150 roadster shown in rear view with the top up.
Similarity to XK 140 rear design is very evident here. Author photo.

XK 150, XK 150 S

ENGINE

Type: dohc in-line 6-cylinder

Bore x Stroke, mm: 83x106 (3.4L), 87x106 (3.8L)

Displacement: 3442 cc (3.4L), 3781 cc (3.8L)

Valve Operation: camshaft

Compression Ratio: 7:1, 8:1, 9:1 (S)

Carburetion: twin SU, triple SU (S)

Bhp (Mrf): 190, 210 (Sp. Eq.), 250 (S)

CHASSIS & DRIVETRAIN

Transmission: 4-speed synchromesh (except first), overdrive on S models and optional automatic transmission

Rear Suspension: semielliptical spring

Gear Ratio: 3.54, 4.54, 6.58, 11.91:1; 3.18, 4.09, 5.247, 7.60, 13.81:1 (overdrive, S)

Front Suspension: independent

Frame: cross-braced steel

GENERAL

Wheelbase, inches: 102

Track, front and rear, inches: 51.5

Brakes: Dunlop disc with servo-assist

Tire Size, front and rear: 16-inch (Dunlop RS-4)

Wheels: wire, pressed-steel optional (rare)

Body Builder: Jaguar Cars Ltd.

Chassis Serial Numbers:

Fixed-head coupe (RHD) 824001 on (1957-61) (LHD) 834001 on (1957-61)

Drop-head coupe (RHD) 827001 on (1957-60) (LHD) 837001 on (1957-60)

Roadster (RHD) 820001 on (1958-60) (LHD) 830001 on (1958-60)

DN suffix indicates that overdrive is fitted

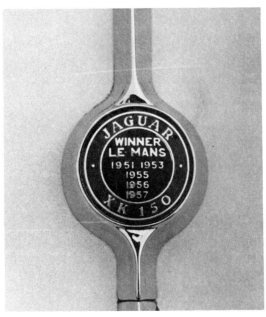

Luggage compartment of XK 150. Note solid wraparound bumper with heavier bumper guards. Note also the larger taillight design and dual exhausts ("modified" model).

Trunk emblem with model identification which will quickly identify all XK 150 models. Author photo.

XK 150 fixed-head coupe in a three-quarter view shows the bulkier, fuller appearance. Note the evolution of design in the "greenhouse" area. Author collection.

Dashboard of XK 150 series roadster. Note vertical placement of instrument panel. Author photo.

An XK 150S roadster. Note the small S on the door just behind the mirror. This is an extremely rare and desirable model. Roaring 20's Auto photo.

CHAPTER 6
LARGE SEDANS
1952-1969

The success story of the XK sports cars provided the nucleus for the development of the touring sedan (saloon, to the English). The 3.4 liter engine was maintained on the same chassis and married to an elegantly styled body. The sedan introduced at the Earl's Court Show in October 1950 demonstrated William Lyons' ability to design cars with a specific audience in mind. This car sported full-sized seats and a full trunk. The styling, although somewhat bulky, was graceful and not overstated. The interior size was increased compared to the Mark V and approximated that of the Bentley, the Rolls-Royce and, indeed, was close to a custom-bodied limousine.

The few detractors were rapidly left in the dust of the rally and touring cup victories amassed by these durable, comfortable and fast sedans. The Jaguar literature is replete with detailed accounts of victories on the rally circuit across the European continent during the early and mid-fifties.

The sole reason that the Mark VII failed to sell well in the American market, and thereby achieve the goal that William Lyons had established for the model, was probably the lack of an automatic transmission. Although all other parameters had been satisfied, the American sedan was never really challenged.

However, the potential buyer should try to conceptualize the car in the eyes of the crowds reported to have completely surrounded the Jaguar display at Earl's Court. There had not been a finer looking, more luxurious or more durable car offered anywhere in England or Europe that possessed the style, class and ride at a price that approached prewar figures.

The basic engine for the Mark VII was the 3.4 liter dohc engine. In May of 1954, Jaguar announced the "M" modifications for the Mark VII sedans, which incorporated the use of the 190 bhp C-type engine. The same transmission options were available. The company also offered a "tuning kit" which included high-lift camshafts, steeply domed pistons and the complementary adjustment parts for the competition trade.

A Mark VII sedan. Distinguishing features are the monoschematic color scheme (compare to the Mark VIII and IX), the thin chrome trim surrounding the grille and the two-piece windshield. Author collection.

THE MARK VII, MARK VIIM, MARK VIII, MARK IX

ENGINE
Type: dohc in-line 6-cylinder
Bore x Stroke, mm: 83x106 (Mark VII, VIII), 87x106 (Mark IX)
Displacement: 3442 cc, 3781 cc (Mark IX)
Valve Operation: cam action
Compression Ratio: 7:1, 8:1 (M)
Carburetion: twin SU
Bhp (Mrf): 160, 190 (M), 210 (Mark VIII), 220 (Mark IX)

CHASSIS & DRIVETRAIN
Transmission: 4-speed synchromesh, optional Laycock-de Normanville overdrive unit, Borg-Warner automatic
Rear Suspension: semielliptical
Gear Ratio: 4.27, 5.84, 8.56, 14.4:1; 4.27, 5.17, 7.44, 13.73:1 (M) standard transmission
Front Suspension: independent
Frame: cross-braced steel

GENERAL
Wheelbase, inches: 120
Track, front, inches: 56 (early VII); 57 (M, Mark VIII, Mark IX)
　　　rear, inches: 56½ (early VII); 58 (M, Mark VIII, Mark IX)
Brakes: Girling 2LS hydraulic with servo-assist, Dunlop disc with servo-assist (Mark IX)
Tire Size, front and rear: 6.00x16
Wheels: 16-inch pressed-steel
Body Builder: Jaguar Cars Ltd.

Chassis Serial Numbers:
Mark VII (RHD) 710001 on (1951-57)
　　(LHD) 730001 on (1950-57)
M series (RHD) 750001 on (1955-57)
　　(LHD) 740200 on (1955-57)
Mark VIII (RHD) 760001 on (1956-59)
　　(LHD) 780001 on (1956-59)
Mark IX (RHD) 770001 on (1958-61)
　　(LHD) 790001 on (1958-61)

The Mark VII sedan was produced essentially unchanged and literally unmodified from late 1950 until early 1953, when the major criticism was corrected. The Mark VII's for export sales were equipped with Borg-Warner automatic transmissions. Ultimately, with the development of a Borg-Warner factory in England in 1955, sufficient automatic transmission units were produced to make the option available to the home market. However, in early 1954, the Mark VII's produced for the home market were offered with the option of a Laycock-de Normanville overdrive unit. These units were also offered on export cars so that four drivetrain options were available. The only indication that the Laycock-de Normanville overdrive unit was fitted was the toggle switch on the dashboard between the steering wheel and the driver's door—left on the export (American) models and right on the home (English) models.

The chassis and suspension of the Mark VII had evolved from the XK sports cars. Although the frame was larger and sturdier, the tested rack-and-pinion steering and antisway characteristics made the handling characteristics appreciated by the serious rallye enthusiast. Here, indeed, was the car which could convey your mother-in-law to church on Sunday morning and rallye competitively in the afternoon.

A few styling improvements which readily identify the M series—namely, larger headlight rims, external horn grilles below the headlights and external fog lights—were made. As always, the radio remained an option. The dashboard slot was filled with a small drawer if the radio was not fitted.

THE MARK VIII

After six years of leadership, both in sales and on the racing and touring tracks, the Mark VII was upgraded and dubbed the Mark VIII. Major improvements were made in both the powertrain and cosmetics.

Improved compression ratios, which produced 210 bhp, upgraded the XK engine and became standard equipment. The improved performance allowed the big sedan to hold its place at the top of the touring and sedan racing classes for another three years. Improvements in appearance readily identify the series: a grille revision, adaptation of a one-piece windshield and the addition of a group of standard interior items—a heater, convenience tables that folded out of the rear of the front seats, an electric clock, wool carpets and nylon trunk linings. Further improving the exterior appearance, several two-tone paint schemes became available. The two colors were separated by a chrome rub-strip, which curved gracefully across the fenders. It was reminiscent of the "Lyons line" of the XK series. Additional chrome trim around the windows, doors and hubcaps was noted

The Mark VIII sedan is easily identifiable by the one-piece window with the two-tone color scheme, heavier chrome trim around the grille and leaping Jaguar hood ornament. Identification of the Mark IX is very difficult and can be done only through research of engine serial numbers. Author photo.

on these models. Only 6,212 of these graceful cars were produced and they remain a favorite of Jaguar buffs.

MARK IX

The advent of the 3.8 liter engines pioneered in the XK 150 and XK 150S models provided additional power to keep Jaguar abreast of the Continental competition and at least somewhat in tune with the American horsepower race. In 1959, they were fitted to the Mark VIII and the designation was changed to the Mark IX. The new Dunlop servo-disc braking system was also added again reflecting advances bred from racing experience.

Few changes were introduced in the interior and exterior styling. A set of pictures displayed in Frostick's book, *The Jaguar Tradition,* attests to the difficulty of identifying the respective models from photographs. The sure method is to check the identification plate located on the firewall in the engine compartment.

Suffice it to say that each of the three models with this body was felt to introduce a significant improvement and was greeted as such by the English motoring writers. Perhaps the fitting conclusion to this section is to mention that although any large sedan will still give comfortable and gracious motoring, the rarest of these sedans would be a Mark IX fitted with the optional divider window.

THE MARK X AND THE 420G

As the decade of the sixties began, it became apparent that Jaguar needed a restyled, large luxury sedan which was also capable of better performance. Thus, in late 1961, the Mark X was introduced. The new body shell unmistakably traced its lineage from the SS I sedans through the Mark V and the Mark VII sedans and the Mark II saloons. The larger interior was termed "Edwardian" by one critic but the space and accouterments were rapidly accepted by the public and one still sees Mark X's in daily use.

Following the E-type by a year, many of the technical innovations were also found on the Mark X. The rear suspension was independent and mounted inboard. The improved 3.8 liter engine featured a new manifold and three SU carburetors. Lower compression ratios in combination with conservative gear ratios seemed to solve the chronic tuning problems noted in the XK 150 and XK-E sports models. The early models were delivered with the standard Borg-Warner automatic transmission but the options of standard transmission and standard transmission with overdrive (still lever-operated and mounted on the dashboard) became available later in the model run.

The styling, although unquestionably Jaguar, was being stretched to satisfy the production engineer. The larger size permitted accommodation of six passengers in real comfort. Sir William Lyons (knighted in 1956 for his contributions to England's industrial heritage) again left his touch on the exterior styling,

The rear seat of the Mark VIII sedan, exemplifying the plush interiors that won this car the reputation of being "the poor man's Rolls." Author photo.

Rear three-quarter view of the Mark VIII. Note the twin gas tanks, full rear wheel covers and flowing two-tone paint scheme. Michael Frostick photo.

which transformed what might have been a very lumpy vehicle into a graceful car in the "Lyons line." A new styling feature was the quadruple integrated headlights.

In 1965, the dohc engine was enlarged to 4235 cc and fitted to the Mark X until the end of the model run in 1967. During these last two years, eighteen "limousine" units were delivered. These are identified by their divider windows installed in the rear surface of the front seat. In 1965, electrically operated windows became available, as did air conditioning.

In mid-summer 1966, Jaguar Cars Ltd. merged with British Motor Corporation. The subsequent autumn saw the introduction of the 420G model which was only the Mark X with a new label. However, the buyer/collector should be careful to correctly identify the prospective purchase. The only external change was the addition of a chrome strip along the side styling crease with a true flasher incorporated in the forward end. The 420G was in production for three years and approximately the same number of units appeared as its predecessor the Mark X. Twenty-four "limousine" units were delivered.

THE MARK X AND 420G
ENGINE

Type: dohc in-line 6-cylinder
Bore x Stroke, mm: 87x106 (3.8L), 92.1x106 (4.2L) 1965 on and 420G
Displacement: 3781 cc, 4235 cc
Valve Operation: twin overhead camshaft
Compression Ratio: 7:1 (4.2L and 420G), 8:1 (3.8L), 9:1 (optional)
Carburetion: 3 SU HD-8
Bhp (Mrf): 265

CHASSIS & DRIVETRAIN

Clutch: SDP hypoid bevel (Mark X); Hausserman diaphragm (4.2L and 420G)
Transmission: 4-speed all synchromesh; overdrive or automatic transmission available

Rear Suspension: coil independent
Gear Ratio: 3.54, 4.54, 6.58, 11.95:1
Front Suspension: coil wide pendant
Frame: unitary construction

GENERAL

Wheelbase, inches: 120
Track, front and rear, inches: 58
Brakes: Dunlop servo-assisted disc
Tire Size, front and rear: 7.50x14
Wheels: pressed-steel disc 14-inch
Chassis Serial Numbers:
Mark X: 3.8L (RHD) 300001 on (1961-65)
3.8L (LHD) 350001 on (1961-65)
4.2L (RHD) ID50001 on (1965-67)
4.2L (LHD) ID75001 on (1965-67)
420G: (RHD) GID 53720 on (1966-69)
(LHD) GID 76961 on (1966-69)

Dashboard of a Mark VIII sedan with automatic transmission.
Note the nonstandard radio installation. Author photo.

Engine compartment of a restored Mark VIII
sedan. Author photo.

Mark X right-hand-drive dashboard. Jags Unlimited photo.

The luxurious Mark X sedan featured a spacious rear passenger compartment with polished walnut vanity tables fitted to the rear of the front seats—nothing superfluous, mind you, everything was correct and in good taste. Bob Stone collection.

Limousine divider window installed in Mark X.
Michael Frostick photo.

The 420G sedan is distinguished by the grille bar and the side-warning lights integrated with the side rub-strips. Otherwise the 420G is the same as the Mark X. Author collection.

CHAPTER 7
SMALL SALOONS
1961-1970

2.4, 3.4 ★★
Mark II ★★★
240, 340 ★★
S-Type ★★★★
420 ★★★

Sedan and saloon racing enjoyed great popularity on the Continent during the fifties, as it allowed the family man to own a sedan to transport his wife and children in style during the week and yet compete with it on the weekends. With the availability of 120 mph speeds from the XK engines, it became logical that a medium-sized sedan, which could approach 100 mph in competition, would be desirable. W. M. Heynes, Jaguar's technical director at the time, and his assistants produced an inexpensive model that incorporated the speed and engineering features of the XK sports car series and the comfort and ride of the Mark VII series into a medium-sized sedan. Thus the 2.4 liter saloon was introduced to the public in September 1955, and produced for 1956. These models are occasionally noted as Mark I's but this is an enthusiast's designation not a factory model name.

With uncanny marketing strategy, Jaguar developed the smaller, lighter sedan, which could re-attract several levels of consumers lost with the phase-out of the Mark V and the advent of the Mark VII. The 2.4 liter sedan was directed to the cost-conscious buyer who still wished the quality construction offered by Jaguar.

Although underpowered, the size-to-weight distribution was appropriate for saloon rallying on the Continent, and the 3.4 liter engine option was offered within the year. Handling improvements were made in these cars practically as they evolved. And the six-year production totals prove the overall popularity of these cars.

THE 2.4 LITER SEDAN

The major technical advance added to the Jaguar line in the 2.4 liter saloon was uni-body construction. The major technical revision was the modification of the proven XK in-line six-cylinder engine. The displacement was reduced to 2483 cc by reducing the stroke. This also reduced engine weight by the reduction in the overall height. The decision to proceed with the six-cylinder engine was somewhat difficult, as the four-cylinder block (XK 100) of the same design had been on the drawing board for ten years.

A 3.4 liter sedan of the first series. Note the thick door pillars and lack of chrome trim around windows. Author photo.

The entirely new external appearance was delightfully similar to the companion Mark VIII—graceful lines, covered rear wheel openings and curved grille (obviously related to the grille then popular on the XK 140 sports cars). The interior, although not as plush as in the larger sedans, left little doubt as to its heritage. The burled Circassian walnut veneer on the dashboard and the instrument layout closely mimicked the Mark VIII.

THE 3.4 LITER SEDAN

In early 1957, the logical move of fitting the medium-sized car with the now-proven, larger, faster engine evolved; and the 3.4 liter sedan was introduced. Now, the family man had an honest 120 mph sedan. Late in the model run, the full wheel covers (spats) were replaced by semicircular ones, which improved the rear quarter appearance immensely.

THE MARK II SEDAN

In the fall of 1959, the critics of the dowdy looks of the 2.4 and 3.4 liter saloons were satisfied with the introduction of the Mark II. The 3.8 liter engine was now available and offered along with the 2.4 liter and 3.4 liter. These models were available for seven years and over 83,000 units were delivered.

Body styling was markedly improved by adding bulk to the rear end and expanding the rear window areas. The general appearance of the trim surrounding all windows and rear license plate holders and lights was modernized to produce a more finished design. The immense popularity enjoyed by this model is in large part due to its pleasing appearance coupled with its spritely performance.

Other styling features introduced on the Mark II series included the optional fog/driving lights mounted in the front fenders where the horn grilles had been. Interior appointments now included trays for the rear passengers and increased use of the walnut veneer. Wire wheels were also available as a factory option in either chrome or painted varieties.

The 240 AND 340 SEDANS

Toward the end of the model run, the austerity of the English financial climate and the introduction of the S-series large sedans led to the 3.8 liter engine option being dropped. The resulting two small sedans (saloons) were known respectively as the 240 and the 340. They are distinguished by the characteristic Mark II body but without the fog/driving lamps in the front fenders. The horn grilles were resurrected to cover the holes and the bumpers were thinner. Only 6,000 units were produced as the new sedan designs, which were to culminate in the XJ series, were introduced.

Few problems plagued the small sedans except for rust. The prospective buyer is advised to check this item carefully as most will display rust even with a moderately well-done restoration. Some hidden areas may require a body-off reconstruction to solve the problem.

Dashboard of the 3.4 liter sedan. Note the instrument layout and the "cubbyhole" behind the steering wheel in the dash for storage. Radio is nonstandard. Author photo.

The rear view of the 3.4 liter sedan emphasizing its rather spartan design. Author photo.

THE S-TYPE AND 420 SEDANS

Lord Montagu of Beaulieu, a respected chronographer and noted Jaguar enthusiast, proposed that the genesis of the S-type sedan was the perceived need for a model that offered more than the small saloons to the middle-class buyer and yet retained the luxury features and included the mechanical improvements which were continually introduced. Therefore, the obviously restyled Mark II appeared.

Sporting a redesigned grille, thinner bumpers, hooded headlights and fully integrated wing lights (turn signals), the front appearance was smoother and more attractive. From the rear, the larger trunk projection afforded more storage space as did the addition of dual gas tanks (one housed in each fender).

The interior was essentially that of the Mark II. The S-type was available with the standard selection of engines (3.4 or 3.8 liters) and the three transmission options. A new mechanical feature was independent rear suspension.

In 1967 with the new corporate structure, the S-type was given a facelift that incorporated the grille style of the Mark X and quadruple headlights. This new model was called the 420 to lend continuity to the numerical sedan presentation of the Jaguar line, as the Mark X had been simultaneously redesignated the 420G. The major interior change was the incorporation of the dashboard clock into a centrally located padded roll on the dashboard.

Taken as a group, the changes and variations of styling seen in both the small and the large sedans represent design experiments which culminated in the styling and appearance of the XJ sedan series introduced in 1968 and still being offered in 1984.

The 420S saloon shows the emphasis of its body inherited from the 3.8 Mk II saloon. Note full wheel disc and clearance hub caps. Author collection.

Front view of the 3.8 liter Mark II sedan. Note the round parking lights set low in the fenders and the optional driving lights. The dark (actually amber) lenses of the parking lights identify this car as a "home" car (made for sale in England or Canada). Author photo.

A 3.8 liter Mark II sedan. Note the thin, chrome-covered door pillars and lighter styling appearance. Author photo.

The dashboard arrangement of the 3.8 liter Mark II. Note the improved instrument layout (driver oriented) and the single and larger glove compartment. Author photo.

Front three-quarter view of author's 1964 3.8 liter Mark II sedan. Note increased window area. Fender-mounted rearview mirrors are not standard. The "turned-down" front bumper is often seen on older Jaguar cars. Author photo.

Trunk view of a 3.8 liter Mark II sedan showing the ample space. Note taillight and wraparound bumper styling acknowledging its heritage from the XK 140 and XK 150 sport models. Author photo.

View of the rear seat of a 3.8 liter Mark II sedan. Note the luxurious appointments in this "middle-priced" car. Flasks and flashlight are owner additions. Author photo.

THE SMALL SALOONS—2.4L, 3.4L, MARK II, 240, 340

ENGINE

Type: dohc in-line 6-cylinder
Bore x Stroke, mm: 83x76.5 (2.4L), 83x106 (3.4L), 81x106 (3.8L)
Displacement: 2483 cc (2.4L), 3442 cc (3.4L), 3781 cc (3.8L)
Valve Operation: overhead camshaft
Compression Ratio: 8:1, 7:1 (optional)
Carburetion: twin SU HD-6 (2.4L had 2 Solex carburetors)
Bhp (Mrf): 112 (2.4L), up to 120 (Mark II), 210 (3.4L), 220 (3.8L)

CHASSIS & DRIVETRAIN

Transmission: 4-speed synchromesh, with overdrive options, automatic available
Rear Suspension: semielliptical
Gear Ratio: 4.55, 6.21, 9.01, 15.35:1 (2.4L); 3.54, 4.54, 6.58, 11.95:1 (3.4L, 3.4L Mark II, 3.8L Mark II)
Front Suspension: independent
Frame: unitary

GENERAL

Wheelbase, inches: 92
Track, front, inches: 54⅝; 55 (Mark II)
rear, inches: 50⅝; 53⅝ (Mark II)
Brakes: Lockheed Brakemaster 2LS servo-assisted hydraulic, Dunlop servo-assisted disc (Mark II)
Tire Size, front and rear: 6.40x15
Wheels: pressed-steel, wire optional on Mark II
Body Builder: Jaguar Cars Ltd.

Chassis Serial Numbers:
2.4L (RHD) 900001 on (1956-59)
   (LHD) 940001 on (1956-59)
3.4L (RHD) 970001 on (1957-59)
   (LHD) 985001 on (1957-59)
Mark II 2.4L (RHD) 100001 on (1960-67)
   (LHD) 125001 on (1960-67)
3.4L (RHD) 150001 on (1960-67)
   (LHD) 175001 on (1960-67)
3.8L (RHD) 200001 on (1960-67)
   (LHD) 210001 on (1960-67)
240 (RHD) IJ1001 on (1968-69)
   (LHD) IJ 30001 on (1968-69)
340 (RHD) IJ50001 on (1968)
   (LHD) IJ80001 on (1968)

An example of the S-type sedan. Note the styling evolution from the Mark II sedan. Identification is easily made by the hooded headlight surrounds. Author collection.

A publicity photo showing a 240 sedan. Distinguishing features are the horn grilles in place of the fog/driving lights and the thinner bumpers. The 340 sedan was similar in appearance but had the 3.4 liter engine. Michael Frostick photo.

The dashboard arrangement of the 420 showing its distinguishing feature—the square center-mounted clock. Michael Frostick photo.

The 420 sedan, which is identified by the quadruple, hooded headlights and the grille shape. The wire wheels and sliding sunroof were options. Author photo.

Three small saloons in a line representing a decade of styling progress. Author photo.

THE S-TYPE AND 420 SEDANS
ENGINE
Type: dohc in-line 6-cylinder
Bore x Stroke, mm: 83x106 (S 3.4L), 87x106 (S 3.8L), 92.1x106 (420)
Displacement: 3442 cc, 3781 cc, 4235 cc
Valve Operation: overhead camshaft
Compression Ratio: 8:1, 7:1 (optional), 9:1 (optional on S type)
Carburetion: twin SU HD-6
Bhp (Mrf): 210 (3.4L), 220 (3.8L), 245 (4.2L)
CHASSIS & DRIVETRAIN
Transmission: 4-speed synchromesh, overdrive and automatic available
Rear Suspension: independent
Gear Ratio: 3.54, 4.54, 6.58, 11.95:1 (3.4L, 3.8L); 3.54, 4.7, 7.44, 10.76:1 (4.2L)
Front Suspension: independent

Frame: unitary
GENERAL
Wheelbase, inches: 102 (S), 107⅜ (420)
Track, front, inches: 56¾
    rear, inches: 54¼
Brakes: Dunlop servo-assisted disc
Tire Size, front and rear: 185x15 (Dunlop 6.40-15 RS5)
Wheels: disc, wire optional
Body Builder: Jaguar Cars Ltd., British Motor Corporation (1966)
Chassis Serial Numbers:
3.4L S-Type (RHD) 1B1001
    (LHD) 1B25001
3.8L S-Type (RHD) 1B50001
    (LHD) 1B75001
420 (RHD) 1F1001
    (LHD) 1F25001

What can one say? *Car and Driver* sought the "World's Ten Most Beautiful Cars" and the Jaguar E-type Series One was the overall winner. This manmade piece of machinery was described in terms usually only reserved by "Real Men" for "Real Women": "sensuous," "liquid," "crisp," "stunningly erotic." The design of this car may well have the widest automotive consumer recognition ever achieved. The feelings stirred for the E-type were identical to the enthusiasm for the XK 120 when it appeared at Earl's Court thirteen years earlier.

This automobile, the design zenith of the "Lyons line," has remained unmatched for two decades, as have other Jaguar cars for three and four decades. The sensual grace which generates from its flow of line is at once unique; yet the careful student of design can easily trace the lineage to the hip line of the XK 150 and from there back to the XK 120/140 and ultimately to the prewar SS 100. The design trend can even be seen in the SS I drop-head coupe of 1936.

The E-type model was produced in three groups: Series One, Series Two and Series Three. Some confusion has grown around the models produced during the production switch from Series One to Series Two. Several body changes and a few significant mechanical changes from the Series Two were adapted to the Series One bodies that were still "on the line." Thus, these models were hybrids and termed, appropriately, by enthusiasts, the Series One and One-Half. Jaguar chose to label these units the Series IA but the name given to them by the enthusiasts has become accepted and is used today.

SERIES ONE

In 1961, this totally new design burst on the market like a fresh breath of spring air. The clean and uncluttered lines coupled with 140 mph performance created an immediate best seller. The E-type was offered in the roadster and coupe (fixed-head) models for the first five years of production. (The fixed-head coupe actually was the faster of the two models due to its aerodynamics.) In 1966, in response to the American market pressures again,

A Series One roadster seen with top up. Similar model with top
down in background. Note covered headlights, steep windshield
and taillights above the rear bumper. Author photo.

the 2+2 fixed-head coupe was introduced. This raised the roof line two inches and the length of the car nine inches, providing room in the rear for two children. These three model offerings were available until the advent of the Series Three. The equipment offered on each of the three body styles was essentially the same and standard throughout the model run. Improvements gained from road testing and owner/racer reports were sequentially incorporated to upgrade the durability and the performance of the cars—leading to author Chris Harvey's comment: "There are no two identical Jaguars."

The engine for the Series One was the proven 3.8 liter double overhead cam six-cylinder engine. It was coupled to the same four-speed transmission. This transmission, a legacy from the XK series and soon to be replaced, had no synchromesh in first gear and very stiff shifting in the others. The engine was fitted with three SU HD-8 carburetors equipped with a manual choke. The three carburetors earned the E-type an unsavory reputation because of the constant need for retuning with every American weather (humidity) change. Some early American E-types have been retrofitted with twin SU carburetion-manifold systems (found on early XK 150 models) for easier adjustment. Space considerations prohibited an automatic transmission until the advent of the 2+2 models. An overdrive unit was not offered (although a few prototype E-types exist with this adaptation, according to Harvey).

In October 1964, the 4.2 liter engine was introduced. The engine block was redesigned, the spacing of the cylinders in the block being the most noticeable change. This engine was coupled with a totally synchromeshed gearbox, to the delight of most owners. Major technical improvements were in the clutch and the electrical and cooling systems.

Inside, the 4.2 liter models sported significant changes. The aluminum plates used for dash trims earlier were replaced by flat colors (mostly black). Armrests were placed on the doors and a "goodies" compartment was mounted on the transmission tunnel. Two small but identifying features denoted the 4.2 liter Series One models: The trunk sported a "4.2 Liter" name-plate and the rear door (trunk) hinges were covered. Added refinements in luxury were made at the expense of weight, and top speeds dropped. Some styling changes, such as the headlight changes for example, are alleged to have cost 3 mph in top speed alone.

It is curious to note that even in 1964 when the 4.2 liter was being road tested, fuel consumption of 22 mpg was very favorably commented upon, albeit at the end of the glowing paragraph about the 140+ mph top speeds attained by a 2+2 coupe.

The 4.2 liter Series One cars were better suited to the American (export) market due, in large part, to their improved

Another Series One roadster which shows modifications to owner's preference—namely twin racing mirrors, grille guard and wind wings. Author photo.

driving tolerance and the interior refinements. However, the true driver's car remains the 3.8 liter Series One models and, in particular, the roadster. Its desirability has increased with the passing years and it remains the ultimate choice of most Jaguar collectors for its uncluttered lines. Curiously, although mechanical refinements should have made for improved performance, they did not. The 3.8 liter was reported by most testers to be the same as the 4.2 liter in speed and handling. The bottom-line improvement was the totally synchromeshed transmission, with all of the later series.

The roadster and coupe were two-passenger cars with a small amount of storage space behind the front seat. Demand for additional passenger space produced the longer, roomier 2+2 coupe. Children were comfortable but full-sized adults were still cramped. However, in both models, the rear compartment's panel could be folded down, facilitating access to the trunk and providing good storage space (the first of the "hatchback" cars).

Although the XK-E called the two-seat open sport car a roadster, a more accurate name would be a drop-head coupe or convertible. The top was not removable and actually fit well, affording a comfortable ride in the most inclement of conditions. Roll-up windows, which had become standard in all models with the XK 150 series, were retained.

THE SERIES ONE AND ONE-HALF

In 1968, two major external changes were made in design which anticipated the introduction of the Series Two. The windshield tilt was increased and the headlight presentation changed. The headlights were moved forward three inches and the plastic covers discarded. The smooth lines of the Series One were broken and so were the top achievable speeds, by several mph. Many of these changes were in large part to comply with the American safety regulations but they were also production evolution points along the path from competitive sports car to comfortable touring car.

THE SERIES TWO

In 1969, the first of the Series Two models appeared and, again, many features were changed to improve passenger comfort and to allow compliance with American import safety laws. All at the cost of top speed, lamented the motor media. Sir William Lyons, in his wisdom, identified US market dominance and then manufactured all models for that market even though the English and Continental safety laws were far less stringent.

The exterior appearance now sported two new indicator lights mounted under the outer margins of the front bumpers. Both the front and rear bumpers wrapped farther around the fenders and were heavier, affording better protection. Twin back-up lights replaced the single light, and the rear lights were

View of engine compartment of a 1968 XK-E Series One and One-Half roadster. Note the triple SU carburetors and overflow radiator arrangement. (Front of car is to right of photo).

A Series One coupe shown in a Jaguar publicity photo. This two-seat hardtop is the successor to the fixed-head coupe of XK fame. Note triple windshield wipers, steep windshield angle and enclosed headlights. All are identifying features. Jaguar Cars, Inc., photo.

moved to a new position below the bumpers. The sides of these lights were not flared into the bodywork until the advent of the Series Three models and their unfinished appearance easily identified this model.

The most identifiable change, however, involved the windshield, which was raked toward the rear by an additional seven degrees. The flow of the "Lyons' line" was markedly improved and this change also readily identified the Series Two. Two windshield wipers replaced the three fitted on Series One models. The Series Two models were also distinguished by a larger hood air-intake opening. The knock-off caps on the wire wheels lost their "ears" and thus the trunk equipment gained another piece of equipment to allow removal of the wire wheels. Pressed-steel wheels were an option offered for the first time in six years and, curiously, were more expensive than the wire wheels.

Inside, the American safety influence was again felt: The toggle switches on the dash were replaced by rocker-style switches, a hazard-warning system was added with its additional switch, the interior mirror was mounted on the front window support and the door handles were buried in the doors. For convenience, the glove compartment received a lock, the dash was padded, the heating system was significantly improved and the starter switch was incorporated in the key mechanism—the first Jaguar without a starter push button.

The Series Two was available in all three body styles for its two-year production run. The same chassis was used on the roadster and the fixed-head coupe models, but the 2+2 frame was nine inches longer. This additional space was to be incorporated into all of the Series Three models. Those of us who measure over six feet have been eternally grateful.

THE SERIES THREE

For many years, Jaguar's advance design group had been interested in a V-12 engine. In 1970, as at most times in the history of the automotive engine, the V-12 was a special item and few versions had survived attempts at mass production. The need for a pace-setting improvement to counter the large American V-8's and the exotic Italian machinery finally persuaded Jaguar to replace the 4.2 liter engine with the 5.3 liter V-12. Thus, the Series Three was born. The body style remained similar and a name change to F-type was avoided.

With the advent of the Series Three, only the roadster and the 2+2 coupe models were offered. The longer wheelbase, developed five years earlier for the 2+2, was used for the roadster as well. The ride and handling were softened and the complaint of the owner "not being able to 'feel' the road" was heard for the first time. However, the awesome power generated by the V-12

Detail of the triple-blade wiper system found on Series One and
Series One and One-Half cars.

A side view of an XK-E 2+2 sedan of the Series One vintage. Identifying features are the covered headlights, the steep windshield
and the taillights, which are placed above the bumper line in the
rear deck. Similarly, the parking lights are placed above the bumper line in the front fenders. The chrome strip beneath the windows
on the door identifies the 2+2. Author collection.

engine more than balanced these complaints. The top speed of 146 mph equaled that of the 3.8 liter roadsters and renewed the spark of the enthusiast.

The longer frame, derived from the 2+2 coupe, added mechanical space and allowed the options of power steering and air conditioning to be offered. Additional interior room was achieved by enlarging the footwells. However, the one major problem of all the E series was not really solved—rust. The multiple closed body spaces common to this model made rust hard to detect until too late. Severely ravaged E-types are too frequently seen.

Externally, the Series Three model was easily identified by its egg-crate grille with the gold Jaguar emblem, and the large V-12 badge on the trunk lid. The wheel openings were flared and enlarged to allow the specially designed Dunlop RS 70 tires to make short-radius turns. An additional air scoop was found beneath and slightly behind the grille. The rear lights were now flared into the rear fenders for a far more pleasing effect. However, extra lights for side visibility were added to the front and rear fenders to satisfy the American safety law pressures. They have always appeared as if a child stuck them on "where ever."

Although most Series Three and E-types are found with chrome wire wheels, this was a factory option. The far less common pressed-steel wheels were standard. Other options were air conditioning, whitewall tires, solid state radio and tinted glass. Shades of Detroit. A hard, all-weather removable top was optional and apparently few were delivered, as I have been trying for five years to locate one without success.

The emission control and safety standards continued to constrict the power and efficiency of the E-type in the first half of the seventies. The bumper guards grew by the year and have become an easy way of identifying the production year of a Series Three Jaguar. The 1970 and 1971 cars had small chrome bumpers with small rubber inserts. The 1972 and 1973 cars had front bumpers of more substantial size, which were essentially chrome nerf plates with rubber surrounds. The 1974 models had large and heavy rubber bumpers in front and in back.

The last fifty Series Three E-types produced were completed in February 1975. They were all painted black, which was not a standard color but represented the sentiment of many enthusiasts as the passing of an era.

Rear deck arrangement of the Series One and Series One and
One-Half roadsters. Note taillights above bumper, optional bumper protectors and nonstandard exhausts.

As stunning today as when it was first introduced—the 3.8 liter
XK-E coupe. By the Series Two models the knock-off lugs will
have lost their "ears." Bob Stone collection.

A Series One and One-Half roadster with its characteristic mixture of styling features: the Series One windshield, parking lights and knock-off wire wheel hubs combined with the Series Two exposed headlights and longer hood. Michael Frostick photo.

Dashboard of Series One and Series One and One-Half roadsters. Note the open "cubbyhole," key and starter switch at center of dash and "unsafe" toggle switches (behind bar of steering wheel).

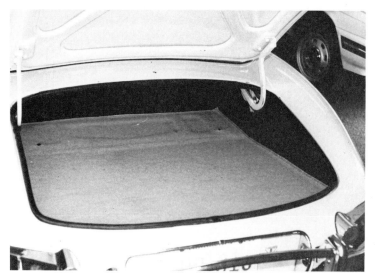

Here's the trunk area for the Series One, Series One and One-Half and Series Two roadsters.

A good example of a Series One and One-Half coupe which combines the steep windshield and the open headlights. Note that the side lights and taillights are still above the bumper guards. In the Series Two, they will appear beneath the bumpers. Author collection.

A composite photo which demonstrates the differences between the Series One and Series Two windshields. Note the difference in the angle formed with the hood. The upper photo is actually a Series One and One-Half (open headlights, side lights and no knock-off wheels) but retains the triple wiper blade arrangement, steep windshield rake and absence of chrome panel on the door. The lower photo is actually a Series Two 2+2 coupe with the longer door. Michael Frostick photos.

Engine compartment of a Series Two 4.2 liter roadster. Note the dohc six-cylinder engine with two carburetors which were standard on this car. Author photo.

E-TYPE SERIES ONE,
SERIES ONE AND ONE-HALF, SERIES TWO
ENGINE
Type: dohc in-line 6-cylinder
Bore x Stroke, mm: 87x106 (3.8L), 92.1x106 (4.2L)
Displacement: 3781 cc, 4235 cc
Valve Operation: twin overhead camshaft
Compression Ratio: 9:1, 8:1 (optional)
Carburetion: triple SU HD-8 (Series One), twin Stromberg CD (Series Two)
Bhp (Mrf): 265 (Series One), 171 (Series Two)
CHASSIS & DRIVETRAIN
Transmission: all-gear synchromesh, available in cars equipped with 4.2L engines. 4-speed synchromesh (in 4.2L), automatic transmission available in 2+2 models (1965)
Rear Suspension: independent
Gear Ratio: 3.31, 4.246, 6.156, 11.177:1
Front Suspension: independent
Frame: unitary with monocoque features
GENERAL
Wheelbase, inches: 96, 105 (2+2)
Track, front, inches: 50, 50¼ (2+2)
rear, inches: 50, 50¼ (2+2)
Brakes: Dunlop servo-assisted
Tire Size, front and rear: 6.40x15, 185x15 (2+2)
Wheels: wire, pressed-steel offered on Series Two models

Body Builder: Jaguar Cars Ltd., British Motor Corp. (1966), British Leyland Motor Corp. (1968)
Chassis Serial Numbers:
Series One
3.8L Roadster (RHD) 850001 on (1961-64) (LHD) 875001 on (1961-64)
Coupe (RHD) 860001 on (1961-64) (LHD) 885001 on (1961-64)
4.2L Roadster (RHD) 1E1001 on (1964-67) (LHD) 1E10001 on (1964-67)
Coupe (RHD) 1E2001 on (1964-67) (LHD) 1E30001 on (1964-67)
2+2 (RHD) 1E50001 on (1964-67) (LHD) 1E75001 on (1964-67)
Series One and One-Half (earliest known)
Roadster (RHD) 1E1864 on (1967-68) (LHD) 1E15889 on (1967-68)
Coupe (RHD) 1E21584 on (1967-68) (LHD) 1E34250 on (1967-68)
2+2 (RHD) 1E50975 on (1967-68) (LHD) 1E77645 on (1967-68)
Series Two
Roadster (RHD) 1R1001 on (1968-71) (LHD) 1R7001 on (1968-71)
Coupe (RHD) 1R20001 on (1968-71) (LHD) 1R25001 on (1968-71)
2+2 (RHD) 1R35001 on (1968-71) (LHD) 1R40001 on (1968-71)

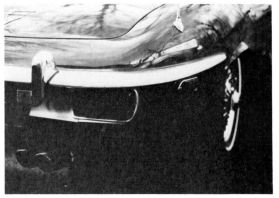

A rear view of the Series Two roadster. Note the lights mounted below the bumper guard but not flared into the fender. Author photo.

Close-up of author's 1973 Series Three rear quarter. Note small rear guards common to 1971-73 cars. Exhaust system is not standard but is an Ansa replacement, which is commonly seen. Author photo.

Examples of 1972 vintage V-12 Series Three automobiles. Both are equipped with the stamped steel wheels rather than the wire wheels. The identifying features here are the egg-crate grille with the chrome surround, which is classical and typical of the Series Three V-12 XK-E's. Author collection.

An early Series Three (V-12 engine) 2+2 coupe. Note the lightweight bumper guards. The pressed-steel wheels seen are most unusual. Roadster in top photo sports the optional removable hardtop. Author and Jaguar Cars, Inc., photos.

THE E-TYPE SERIES THREE

ENGINE
Type: 12-cylinder in V-block (60°)
Bore x Stroke, mm: 90x70
Displacement: 5343 cc
Valve Operation: single overhead camshaft per bank
Compression Ratio: 9:1
Carburetion: 4 Zenith-Stromberg 175 CD2SE
Bhp (Mrf): 250

CHASSIS & DRIVETRAIN
Transmission: 4-speed full synchromesh, automatic available
Rear Suspension: independent wishbone
Gear Ratio: 3.54, 4.92, 6.73, 10.37:1 (standard)
Front Suspension: independent wishbone
Frame: unitary with monocoque features

GENERAL
Wheelbase, inches: 105
Track, front, inches: 54.5
     rear, inches: 53
Brakes: Girling disc servo-assisted
Tire Size, front and rear: Dunlop E70 VR-15
Wheels: 15-inch wire, solid discs optional
Body Builder: British Leyland Motors, Inc.

Chassis Serial Numbers:
Series Three Roadster (RHD) 1S1001 (1971-75)
    (LHD) 1S20001 (1971-75)
2+2 (RHD) 1S50001 (1971-75)
    (LHD) 1S70001 (1971-75)

Close-up of author's 1973 Series Three roadster. Note detail of bumper guard, parking lights, headlights and wire wheel hubs. Author photo.

A 1973 Series Three 2+2 coupe. Note the heavier front bumper guards of chrome and rubber. Wire wheels are common. Author photo.

Close-up of 1974 Series Three rear bumper. Note the massive guards. The exhaust system is standard. Author photo.

Dashboard of a Series Three with factory-installed air conditioning mounted below wooden steering wheel (which is not standard). Author photo.

A 1974 Series Three roadster fitted with the optional factory hard top. Note the massive bumper guards. *E-Jag* photo.

Dashboard of a Series Three roadster without air conditioning installed. Author photo.

Engine compartment of an unrestored Series Three V-12 roadster. Expect to see this level of condition in most unrestored engines. Author photo.

<table>
<tr><td>CHAPTER 9
**THE XJ SERIES
SEDANS AND COUPES
1968-1988**</td><td>XJ6 1968-1972 ★★★
XJ6 Series Two 1972-1977 ★★★
XJ6L Series Two 1972-1979 ★★★
XJ12 Series Two 1972 ★★★★★★
XJ12L Series Two 1972-1978 ★★★★
XJ6 Series III 1979-1987 ★★★★
XJ6 1988-
XJ6C ★★★★
XJ12C ★★★★★</td></tr>
</table>

THE XJ SEDANS

In 1968, Jaguar's design exercises which had occurred in sedan styling in the previous fifteen years culminated—the XJ sedan was introduced and with it significant technical improvements.

The unitary frame was redesigned to give it three "boxes" for enhanced rigidity. The suspension was given antinosing properties, and power steering was made standard equipment on the 4.2 liter units. Girling servo-assisted brakes and rack-and-pinion steering improved the handling of the XJ sedan. The significant choice given the prospective home-market buyer was the option of a 2.8 liter version of the famous six-cylinder engine.

The new style of the XJ sedans produced an unmistakable image. The car appeared lower and wider and more aerodynamic. The one styling feature dropped from this design was the nip in the rear roof/window line which was a hallmark of the Jaguar sedan for three decades. However, the window styling retained the "watch."

In 1972, the long-rumored V-12 engine was introduced and the Series Two was born. Immediately, all the previous XJ models were unofficially designated Series One. Coupled with this enthusiastically received addition, the long-wheelbase model, designated the "L," made four options now available. This latter modification became so popular that the short-wheelbase model was dropped in 1977.

It should be noted that a few "short-wheelbase 12's" exist. Near the end of the model run, a few Series One sedans were factory delivered with the V-12 engine. Although they seem overpowered, the driving experience is exciting. They are the rarest of the XJ Series models and are identified by the Series II grille mounted in the Series I car.

The fuel crises of the late seventies and the increasing requirements for emissions control ultimately forced the V-12 sedan from the American market in mid-1978. However, the reliability and economy of the venerable dohc six-cylinder engine,

Note the identifying letters and numbers on this 1971 unrestored XJ6 sedan belonging to the author. Dual exhausts are standard through 1987. Author photo.

A Series One XJ6 sedan. Note styling lineage from the 420 and the low roof line. The grille design is the distinguishing feature for the XJ sedans. Jaguar Cars, Inc., photo.

first introduced over thirty-five years ago, continues to attract buyers today.

In 1979, the now well-recognized long-wheelbase style was given a "facelift" and designated the Series Three. The changes were hard to detect but the grille design, heavier bumpers and new rear light layouts were identifiers. The significant change was, however, almost unnoticeable except by the real experts: the raising of the roof line. This change increased interior headroom and visibility.

The interior of the XJ sedan retained the burled walnut and Connolly hide and the classic Jaguar dashboard. By now, most of the technical features were standard equipment; the only choices one needed to make were those of interior and exterior color.

The buyer of the used Jaguar XJ sedan is referred to the right rear panel adjacent to the license plate. Here is found the designation of the model, the engine and the wheelbase—XJ 6 or 12 and XJ6L or 12L. The 2.8 liter cars, delivered only in Europe, are also identified in the same place.

The buyer who chooses a car from England or the Continent, or who finds a right-hand-drive (RHD) car in another country, is cautioned to check the emission-control adaptation before transporting the car to the United States. Conversion may be costly, although the rarity and the assumed economy of the 2.8 liter sedan may seem desirable.

From 1983 through 1987, the quality of the XJ6 sedan demonstrated a steady improvement. With quality came the reliability so desired by both Jaguar owners and builders. By 1985, Jaguar offered a three-year/30,000 mile warranty on all of its cars.

The models change little from year to year except for slight changes in exterior color. In 1986, for the US market, a high-level stop light was added to the rear window. This will easily identify the 1986 and 1987 sedans. Industry improvements in audio systems were serially incorporated, and in the 1987 model a theft alarm was included.

In 1982, the luxury Vanden Plas sedan editions were introduced. The noticeable features were specially matched Connolly hides allowing a different seat pattern which is reminiscent of the sports seats of earlier models. Special burled wood panels were used on the interior and placed on the console surface. Reading lights and rear headrests were in the rear compartment. A special identification plaque replaced the XJ6 letters on the right rear trunk panel; two-color accent stripes appeared on the "hip" line. Although *Road & Track* suggested in a 1983 review that the extras were probably worth the investment, by 1986 little difference existed between the two models, and indeed color choices

Dashboard of Series One XJ sedan. All features are standard equipment throughout the XJ line. Author photo.

A Series Two (V-12 engine) XJ sedan. Note the new grille and the heavier bumper. Pressed-steel wheels are standard throughout the series but change design with the Series Three. Author photo.

were wider in the XJ6 selections. The Vanden Plas interior was restricted to two choices and neither was coordinated well with the dash cover and headlines.

1988 XJ6 AND VANDEN PLAS

In mid-1987 the first new Jaguar design since the XJ-S and the first new sedan in twenty years were appearing in American showrooms. The motoring public, both consumer and press, eagerly awaited this event and European driving reports by *Road & Track* and *Automobile* only heightened the anticipation.

In 1982, Jaguar was allowed to become an independent company again under the stewardship of John Egan. A product reputation for poor workmanship and unreliability of mechanicals existed in the sedans and the sports models. Egan directed a two-pronged plan to attack this problem: development of a totally new car and specific attention to quality improvement in the XJ6 and XJ-S. By 1986, quality and reliability were competitive with American luxury cars and a three-year/30,000 mile warranty (unheard of for Jaguar) helped to spur sales to record levels.

While all of this was going on, the "XJ40" project was progressing—a totally new sedan with enough luxury to equal Mercedes-Benz, and enough performance to surpass all sedans in production. Interestingly enough, the XJ6 designation was retained for product recognition.

Following a model as loved as the Series III XJ6, the 1988 XJ6 sedan will invite comparisons, and a lot of personal feelings will be expressed. However, having driven both an XJ6 and a Vanden Plas, there is no question, in my mind, that the 1988 XJ6 is a superior driving machine. Although not much larger, the car looked longer and lower, and handles like it. Actually, driving the car is very reminiscent of the experience of driving a Mark X or 420G sedan. The interior is larger and its finish better. State-of-the-art electronics and gadgets are equivalent to other foreign and American cars.

The engine is entirely new: a 3.6L all-aluminum 6-cylinder block with four valves per cylinder. Other unique engineering features include low ground-live switching reducing voltage at the switch from 12 to 5, which should greatly increase reliability, wiring connectors built to aircraft specifications, and multiple microprocessor monitoring systems. Antilock braking systems are standard equipment and the all new suspension system is an improved, fully independent system. The ride and handling is smooth and sure.

The Vanden Plas model is $4,000 more, for which the proud owner again gets tables in the rear compartment (not seen since the Mark X sedan and the S saloons). The leather is distinctly better; the carpets are deeper; and the heated driver seat, external mirrors, door locks and headlight washers are unique. One major engineering exclusive offered on the Vanden Plas is a limited-slip differential. As has become traditional, special exterior paints and the two interior colors are offered. One subtle driver convenience is a left foot rest—unique and most welcome. All in all, the Vanden Plas seems to be well worth the extra money this year for the first time.

It is curious, however, that such amenities as lighted vanity mirrors, interior trunk releases and wire wheel options have not been adopted; and, a good red leather interior would seem to be a good seller; and . . . my wife still likes the traditional look of the Series III.

But, as each automotive writer has said so far, it is a better all-around automobile, and I predict it will sell well. The SOS (Service-on-Site) should also be a unique feature, which, if implemented well, will attract buyers, as it is offered for no extra charge on all 1988 Jaguar cars.

THE XJ COUPE

The lure of factory team competition remained in the minds of the Jaguar management people. In 1974, a two-door coupe version of the popular XJ sedan appeared. The short-wheelbase frame with either the 4.2 liter six-cylinder engine or the 5.3 liter twelve-cylinder engine was covered by a beautiful coupe body. The ultimate intent for this coupe was competition against the BMW and other coupes on the Continental touring car circuit. But the dream was not to be. For as beautiful as the coupe was, the problem of excess weight was never solved and its competitive record rarely rose higher than second. The coupe was dropped from production in mid-1978 after a total production run of only 1,676 cars.

However, with the passage of time, the balance and beauty of the XJ6 or XJ12C have maintained popularity and desirability. The XJ12C has become the rarest of the production-run Jaguars and is now very desirable.

XJ6 SEDAN AND COUPE 2.8L, 4.2L

ENGINE
Type: dohc in-line 6-cylinder
Bore x Stroke, mm: 83x86 (2.8L), 92x106 (4.2L)
Displacement: 2792 cc (2.8L), 4235 cc (4.2L)
Valve Operation: dual overhead camshaft
Compression Ratio: 9:1 (4.2L)
Carburetion: 2 SU dual Zenith-Stromberg
Bhp (Mrf): 140 (2.8L), 170 (4.2L)

CHASSIS & DRIVETRAIN
Transmission: automatic; 4-speed synchro-mesh with overdrive (optional)
Rear Suspension: independent
Front Suspension: independent
Frame: box-construction, unitary

GENERAL
Wheelbase, inches: 109, 113 (L models), 109 (coupe)
Track, front, inches: 58
      rear, inches: 58
Brakes: Girling disc
Tire Size, front and rear: 18.5×15, 20.5×15
Wheels: pressed-steel
Body Builder: British Leyland Motors, Inc.

Chassis Serial Numbers:
XJ6 1969 1L 50001 on
    1970 1L 53203 on
    1971 1L 55686 on
    1972 1l 64129 on
    1973 UD1L 6990BW on
    1974 UE2N 50001BW on
XJ6L 1974 UE2T 50093BW on
    1975 UF2T 54779 on
    1976 UG2T 56746BW on
    1977 UH2T 63599
    1978 UJ2T 69451BW
    1978½ JAVLN 48C 100001 to year end (FED, CALIF)
    1979 JAVLN 49C 100749
XJ6 Series Three 1979 JAVLN 49C 300001 on
    1980 JAVLN 4 AC 310676 on
    1981 SAJAV 134 BC 320092 on
    1982 SAJAV 134 CC 330273 on
    1983 SAJAV 134 DC 346688 on
    1984 SAJAV 134 EC 366290 on
    1985 SAJAV 134 FC 389879 on
    1986 SAJAV 134 GC 431604 on
    1987 SAJAV 134 HC 461709 on
XJ6C 1975 UF2J 50045 BW on
    1976 UG2J 51369 BW on
    1977 UH2J 52842 BW on
Vanden Plas 1982 SAJAY 134 CC 330273 on
    1983 SAJAY 134 DC 346688 on
    1984 SAJAY 134 EC 366290 on
    1985 SAJAY 134 FC in series
    1986 SAJAY 134 GC In series
    1987 SAJAY 134 HC in series

1988 XJ6 SEDAN

ENGINE
Type: 6-cylinder all-aluminum in-line block
Bore × Stroke, mm: 91×92
Displacement: 3590 cc (3.6L)
Valve Operation: dual overhead camshaft (3.6×3.6, 4 valves per cylinder)
Compression Ratio: 8.2:1
Carburetion: fuel injection, Lucas micro-processor system
Bhp (Mrf): NA

CHASSIS AND DRIVETRAIN
Transmission: 4-speed automatic 2F with J-gate shift selector
Rear Suspension: independent
Front Suspension: independent
Frame: box-construction, unitary

GENERAL
Wheelbase, inches: 113.0
Track, front, inches: 59.1
    rear, inches: 59
Brakes: hydraulic, power-boost outboard-mounted disc with ABS braking system
Tire Size: front and rear 18.5×15
Body Builder: Jaguar Cars, Ltd.

Chassis Serial Numbers:
XJ6 SAJHV 154 JC 506664 on
XJ6 Vanden Plas SAJKV 154 JC in series

Rear view of Garry Brody's Series One XJ6L. Note series identification letters on the right. This is common to all XJ's. Author photo.

A composite photo showing the rear quarter treatment of a 1981 XJ6 (top) and 1984 XJ6 (bottom). The 4.2 denoting engine size has been deleted. Compare with the 1971 XJ6 and 1976 XJ6L.

The 1978 XJ12 was designated as the best car in the world by the British magazine *Car*. it came standard with the air conditioning, power brakes and windows and leather upholstery on all seats. Jaguar Cars, Inc., photo.

Engine compartment of a 1984 XJ6.

A Series Three (after 1979 all dohc six-cylinder engines). Note the grille arrangement, higher roof line and enlarged bumper. Author photo.

Identifying features on the Series Three sedans, introduced for the 1980 model year, are a new grille and larger greenhouse. The windshield is also more slanted and the front quarter vent windows have been eliminated. Bob Stone collection.

Rear view of a Series Three. Note slightly altered rear light grouping and higher roof line. Compare also the distinguishing rear letters. Author photo.

A composite photo of the dashboard of a 1981 XJ6 (top) and a
1984 XJ6 (bottom) showing the addition of the on-board trip
computer. The clock is replaced by a leaping Jaguar symbol.
Author photo.

Dashboard and console arrangements of 1988 XJ6. Note button panels behind steering wheel, J-style gear shift lever and seat-adjustment levers on side of console. Author photo.

The 1988 XJ6 in front three-quarter view. Note the strong evolutionary design trend linking the XJ6 Series III and earlier sedan models. Jaguar Cars, Inc., photo.

View of 1988 XJ6 trunk layout. Note bumper containing rear lights and side lights. Dual exhausts are standard. Author photo.

Driver's door layout with "puddle" light.

XJ12 SEDAN AND COUPE

ENGINE
Type: 12-cylinder in V-block (60°)
Bore x Stroke, mm: 90x70
Displacement: 5343 cc
Valve Operation: single overhead camshaft per cylinder bank
Compression Ratio: 7.8:1
Carburetion: 4 Zenith-Stromberg 175 CD2SE, Lucas fuel injection (later models)
Bhp (Mrf): 250

CHASSIS & DRIVETRAIN
Transmission: 3-speed automatic, 4-speed total synchromesh
Rear Suspension: independent
Gear Ratio: 3.54, 5.13, 8.46, 16.92:1
Front Suspension: independent
Frame: 3 box unitized

GENERAL
Wheelbase, inches: 109 (short models and coupe), 113 (L models)

Track, front, inches: 58
    rear, inches: 58 1/3
Brakes: Girling disc
Tire Size, front and rear: 205x15
Wheels: pressed-steel
Body Builder: British Leyland Motors, Inc.

Chassis Serial Numbers:
XJ12 1973 U01P 50153 on
XJ12L 1974 UE2R 50001 BW on
    1975 UF2R 53930 BW on
    1976 UG2R 54264 BW on
    1977 UH2R 56786 on
    1978 UJ2R 58421 BW on
    1978½ JBVLV48C 100001 on (FED)
    JBVLX48C 100001 on (CALIF)
XJ12 III I 1979 JBVLN49C 300001 on
XJ12C 1975 UF2G 50060 BW on
    1976 UG2G 50426 BW on

XJ12C two-door coupe. These well-balanced lines have been ac-centuated by an owner-added chrome rub-protection-strip. All coupes came factory-equipped with black vinyl tops. Author photo.

THE XJ-S

In February 1975, the last of the celebrated E-types rolled off the assembly line. This black beauty was transported to the Jaguar factory collection to take its rightful place alongside the beautiful bronze XK 120 roadster that first appeared in 1948 at Earl's Court. Several months later, the long-anticipated "new" Lyons design was introduced—the XJ-S. Its great interest, and perhaps its greatest claim to fame, was its distinction of being the last sports car designed by Sir William Lyons.

Mechanically, the proven 5.3 liter V-12 engine equipped with fuel injection was standard. The frame and suspension were basically those designed for the E-type, refined for the XJ sedan series and now adapted to the new sports touring body style. The steering which was power-assisted was made more responsive for high-speed handling by reducing the turn (lock-to-lock) ratios. Dunlop again specifically designed tires for this model.

Styling, although unmistakably Lyons, was new and different for Jaguar. Aerodynamic features were added from extensive wind tunnel testing. A spoiler was fitted under the front bumper as was an undershield beneath the engine, which improved overall handling and reduced drag. Both of these items were always standard equipment. Sir William Lyons is quoted by writer Paul Skilleter as saying that aesthetic considerations "gave way" to aerodynamic needs.

The closed-coupe sports car concept was basically a result of two factors: The safety laws enacted in the United States made the production of a drop-head coupe (convertible) fiscally impractical, and the marketing demand appeared to indicate the need for a high-speed, luxury, grand touring car. Hence the design.

However, the "wind-in-the-hair crowd" still desired a convertible, and two manufacturers (one on each side of the Atlantic) began conversions. Long waiting lists for XJ-S convertibles quickly formed.

The interior appointments were upgraded in 1988. More leather replaced vinyl in non-seat locations such as the steering wheel. Burled wood was returned to dashboard insets and door cappings. In 1984, a dash-mounted on-board trip computer became standard equipment and the audio equipment has been upgraded on a yearly basis.

The HE (high efficiency) engine was introduced in 1982 and featured a new Fireball (high-swirl) combustion chamber which gave better fuel consumption, thus raising the V-12 efficiency ratio from 9-10 mpg to 15 mpg in city driving. It also improved emission control values.

THE XJ-SC

Jaguar Cars has introduced a cabriolet which retains the XJ-S look and line but the top folds down. The "targa"-like struts which remain are unsightly. But a new feature is a significantly modified engine, the AJ6, which ultimately became the standard engine in the 1988 XJ6 sedan; however, the US-delivered cars are fitted with the 5.3L HE V-12 engine. The AJ6 is a six-cylinder engine built new from the crankshaft to the twenty-four valves. The block is aluminum and the "May heads" (Fireball combustion chambers) have been adapted. *Road & Track* assessed the pros and cons and concluded that the engine produces the same end result as the V-12 engine: 0-60 mph in 7.6 seconds.

The cabriolet (XJ-SC) has remained essentially the same as this is written in early 1987. The ungainly top can be set in eight different combinations but changing from the rear hardtop to soft top is a two-hour project with tools. The soft parts will store in the trunk but at the expense of almost all the storage space. Similarly, the inside rear seats, which, although small, are present in the coupe (2+2), removed in the SC. A luggage rack replaces the space. The finish of the materials is good and the seals reported satisfactory. The increased stiffening has raised the curb weight to 4,040 pounds, higher than the sedan.

THE CONVERTIBLE

As noted above, Custom Coachcrafters designed full convertibles. In 1986, Jaguar Cars authorized and marketed a custom-made convertible crafted by Hess and Eisenhardt. The lines of the car are actually improved by the convertible style with the top either up or down. Personal inspection of two of these cars has convinced me of the superb quality built into these modifications. This factory-authorized conversion is done in the United States on standard XJ-S coupes after importation. Thus, the company-sold convertibles are not identifiable by serial numbers.

The 1976 Jaguar XJ-S. Bob Stone collection.

On the front view of an XJ-S of 1982 vintage, note the addition of the front air deflector ("dam") under the bumper. Rear three-quarter view of a 1975 XJ-S, which is distinguished by the design of the wheel discs. Note XJ-S letters on the right trunk panel. Jaguar Cars, Inc., photo.

Engine compartment of the XJ-S, which were all equipped with the V-12 engine. Author photo.

The convertible modification of the XJ-S as interpreted and executed by Custom Coachcraft of Bellevue, Washington. Custom Coachcraft photo.

The dashboard of the 1984 Jaguar showing the in-dash trip computer. Bob Stone collection.

XJ-S, XJ-SC, CONVERTIBLE

ENGINE

Type: 12-cylinder in V-block (60°)
Bore x Stroke, mm: 90x70
Displacement: 5343 cc
Valve Operation: single overhead camshaft
per cylinder bank
Compression Ratio: 9.5:1, 11.5:1 (HE)
Carburetion: Lucas/Bosch fuel injection,
Lucas digital fuel injection
Bhp (Mrf): 262

CHASSIS & DRIVETRAIN

Transmission: 3-speed automatic (GM Turbo
Hydra-matic), 4-speed total synchromesh
(available in England)
Rear Suspension: independent with coil
springs
Gear Ratio: 3.07, 4.54, 7.61, 18.27:1
Front Suspension: independent
Frame: unitized with monocoque features

GENERAL

Wheelbase, inches: 102
Track, front, inches: 58.62
rear, inches: 58.65
Brakes: Girling power-assisted disc
Tire Size, front and rear: 205x15

Wheels: cast alloy steel 15x70VR15
Body Builder: British Leyland Motors, Inc.

Chassis Serial Numbers:
1976 UF2W 50001 BW on
    UG2W 50168 BW on
1977 UH2W 52727 on
1978 UJ2W 54673 on
1978½ JNVEV48C 100001 on
1978½ JNVEX48C 100001 on
1979 JNVEV49C 100234 on
1980 JNVEV 4 AC 104236 on
1981 N/A
1982 SAJNV584 CC 105338 on
1983 SAJNV 584 DC 107988 on
1984 SAJNV 584 EC 112232 on
Cabriolet serial numbers N/A

XJ-S

1985 SAJNV	584FC	117339		on
1986 SAJNV	584GC	125020		on
1987 SAJNV	584HC	134286		on
1988 SAJNV	584JC	139052		on

XJ-SC

1985 SAJNV	384FC	in series
1986 SAJNV	384GC	in series
1987 SAJNV	384HC	in series
1988 SAJNV	384JC	in series

The 1984 XJ-SC cabriolet with the top in the "landau" position. The remainder of the canvas top can be lowered. The first "American" model deliveries were scheduled for July 1984. Author collection.

1987 Jaguar XJ-S cabriolet showing top in the fully down, soft arrangement. Note center bar and 1987 high-level stop light on trunk. Jaguar Cars, Inc., photo.

Rear three-quarter view of XJ-SC with hardtop arrangement in place. Author photo. Car courtesy Keelor Motor Car.

Jaguar XJ-S convertible with coachwork by Hess and Eisenhardt.

Late in the fifties, the need for expansion of Jaguar's production space had already led to the purchase of an unused Daimler factory and the purchase of the entire company was shortly to follow. Daimler, at that time, was noted for a good V-8 engine and it was natural for Lyons to utilize it. The marriage of the Mark II body and the V-8 engine led to a production run of over 17,000 units.

The main difference between the Jaguar Mark II and the Daimler V-8 and V-8/250, other than the engine, was found only in the grille. The outer chrome shell was heavier, both in construction and appearance. It was typified by vertical grooves on the top of the grille surround. This has remained the identifying feature to date.

In 1967, the 420 unit was marketed under the Daimler trademark as the Sovereign model with only the grille design to distinguish the two. In 1969, the model was upgraded to the new XJ body and the sole distinguishing feature remained the different grille and marque plates. When the V-12 engine became available, the Daimler sedans were fitted with it and dubbed the Double-Six. Daimler models were also given the coupe body to market under similar names. In general, the production runs for Daimler models were about one-fourth of those for Jaguar cars. This marketing strategy continues to the present. The Daimler Double-Six coupe, with a production run of only 408 units, certainly is a collector item of unrecognized potential.

Through 1987, Daimler Double-Six versions of the XJ6 were made and marketed throughout England. Some models have found their way to the United States via the "gray market." Although rare in the United States, they are not necessarily collectible.

VANDEN PLAS

Throughout the seventies, several unfinished Jaguar units were delivered each year to the independent coachbuilder Vanden Plas. Some of the bodies fitted were custom units but some were marketed as "landaulettes" during the years 1974 and 1975. These

An early Daimler based on the Mark II sedan body but utilizing the Daimler V-8 engine in early models. Note the *fluted* grille surround. Michael Frostick photo.

The Daimler modification of the 420 sedan. Michael Frostick photo.

custom units do not include the Jaguar limousine models with the window dividers.

In 1982, Jaguar offered an exercise "in pure indulgence" —the Vanden Plas luxury *model*. The Connolly hides were specially selected for smoothness and freedom from blemishes and placed over a heavier seat pad. Individually operated map lights in the rear and heavier pile carpeting throughout were additional features. The 1983 models were available in only two colors—sable or silver sand. Unfortunately, as noted above, the only engine available was the fuel-injected 4.2 liter dohc six-cylinder. However, *Road & Track* was suitably impressed and implied that "it might be worth the extra cost." However, it should be understood that this Vanden Plas model is only a marketing upgrade.

E-Jag magazine has recently shown photographs of a custom sedan produced for Harrod's (a quality English department store). It is not known whether this is intended to be a production model or is merely an advertising item.

A Daimler "Double-Six" distinguished by the grooves in the chrome surrounding the grille and the name on the trunk panel. Michael Frostick photo.

The most luxurious of Jaguars, the Vanden Plas production model. Shown here is a 1982 model. Bob Stone collection.

Special 1984 Jaguar sedan produced for Harrod's. Metal trim is gold-colored and wheel discs are custom made. *E-Jag* photo.

The interior of the 1982 Vanden Plas is both restrained and sumptuous. Painstaking attention to fitting and detail is the car's hallmark. Bob Stone collection.

View of the rear seat compartment of the Harrod's Jaguar. Note built-in television and curtains. *E-Jag* photo.

THE XK-C

In 1950, the XK 120's being raced by private owners were establishing an excellent record. These privately prepared cars had even finished exceedingly well at Le Mans, the pinnacle of sports car racing of that era. William Lyons and his coworkers at Jaguar had always been intrigued with the idea of factory-supported and -sponsored racing teams. The two concepts ultimately led to the creation of a competition version of the XK 120—the XK-C, or C-type.

The 3.4 liter dohc engine underwent several modifications to the cylinder head (redesigned ports and variations in head design), which ultimately led to the "C" (red) head mentioned earlier. The gearbox and drivetrain were placed in a new frame designed of steel tubing to provide additional strength but with less weight. The driver's cockpit was enclosed by the monocoque structure which supported a new body designed only for racing. Unique to this racer, the hood hinged forward for easy access to the engine compartment and the rear sheetmetal could be removed as one panel.

Jaguar authority Andrew Whyte lists the entire production run of the XK-C as fifty-three cars; thus, next to the XK-SS, this may be the rarest of all Jaguars. There seems to be a certain heritage in the XK-C which links it with the large prewar open racing cars one had to "drive, not handle." However, it attained its own preeminence with the 1953 overall win at Le Mans. Jaguar was now fully in the business of "works sports car racing."

THE D-TYPE

The successes of the XK-C at Le Mans in 1951 and 1953 encouraged William Lyons and Malcolm Sayer to improve their designs; and the second "built-for-competition" Jaguar was born: the D-type.

The durable in-line six-cylinder engine was modified for long-distance endurance racing (Le Mans) and reworked to allow it to be tilted into the engine compartment of the new body design.

The rare and beautiful C-type. *Jaguar Journal* photo.

The XK-C or C-type of the early fifties. Author collection.

Malcolm Sayer provided an aerodynamic body to cover the monocoque frame, which was designed specifically for the D-type.

In its first competitive effort, the works D-type achieved 172.9 mph and a second-place finish. The lessons learned, however, were incorporated into the next series of models and the "long-nose" versions appeared. In 1955, the works D-type won Le Mans, beginning a string of three successive victories. In late 1955, the D-type went into full production, rolling down an assembly line paralleling those for the Mark VII and the XK 140 models. The short-nose version accounted for seventy-one cars and the long-nose for six units.

Many D-types were modified for various racing tasks by the works and also by private owners. It may be somewhat difficult to ascertain what is truly original for any given D-type without significant investigation. The effort, however, would be worthwhile as this is an extremely desirable model.

THE XK-SS
The successes of the D-type bred instant recognition of the shape. The long snout and the distinctive, offset airfoil identified the best racing car in the world. It was obvious Jaguar should capitalize on this product popularity. Near the end of 1956, the XK-SS arrived on the scene.

The basic short-nose D-type body was modified to accommodate a top and side-curtains, a door added on the driver's side, the passenger compartment enlarged and connected, and the headrest removed. Its performance and handling left little doubt of its heritage. It was a machine to go to the grocery store in as well as to go racing.

Unfortunately, the factory fire in February 1957 effectively stopped production of the XK-SS with only eighteen models. Production equipment, much of it handmade, was never replaced. All efforts were directed to restoring production of the sports cars and the sedans. And, after all, the E-type was already on the drawing boards.

THE JAGUAR SEDANS, MARK VII TO MARK 2
Most of the sedans produced by the Jaguar factory were suitable for some kind of competition, particularly so in the fifties and sixties. Obviously, most of the factory-supported activity took place in England and the rest of Europe, and the greatest successes came on the racetrack rather than in rallying. Many race fans, now likely to be fifty or more years old, can remember the excitement of Moss passing Tony Rolt at Silverstone in 1954, both in Mark VIIs.

Four years later, Mike Hawthorn could be seen stretching adhesion past the limit in a 3.4 liter Mark 1. In 1960 and 1961 the 3.8 Mark 2 swept the field with the big names: Salvadori, Graham

The D-type (long-nose version). Michael Frostick photo.

C-TYPE

ENGINE
Type: dohc in-line 6-cylinder
Bore x Stroke, mm: 83x106
Displacement: 3442 cc
Valve Operation: double overhead camshaft
Compression Ratio: 9:1
Carburetion: twin SU horizontal with special cylinder head
Bhp (Mrf): 200

CHASSIS & DRIVETRAIN
Transmission: 4-speed standard synchromesh
Rear Suspension: rigid with trailing links
Gear Ratio: 3.31, 3.99, 5.78, 9.86:1
Front Suspension: independent
Frame: Steel tubing with monocoque features

GENERAL
Wheelbase, inches: 96
Track, front and rear, inches: 51
Brakes: Lockheed 2LS hydraulic drum brakes
Tire Size, front and rear: 6.00x16 (6.50x16 optional)
Wheels: wire
Body Builder: Jaguar Cars Ltd.
Chassis Serial Numbers:
001 to 0053

D-TYPE

ENGINE
Type: in-line 6-cylinder
Bore x Stroke, mm: 83x106
Displacement: 3442 cc
Valve Operation: double overhead camshaft
Compression Ratio: 9:1
Carburetion: 3 twin-choke Weber DC03
Bhp (Mrf): 250

CHASSIS & DRIVETRAIN
Transmission: 4-speed synchromesh
Rear Suspension: independent
Gear Ratio: 3.54, 4.82, 5.82, 7.61:1 (many options)
Front Suspension: independent
Frame: monocoque, steel tube

GENERAL
Wheelbase, inches: 90
Track, front, inches: 50
  rear, inches: 48
Brakes: Dunlop disc
Tire Size, front and rear: 6.50x16
Wheels: alloy discs with center lock
Body Builder: Jaguar Cars Ltd.
Chassis Serial Numbers:
401 to 406 (1954)
501 to 573 (1955-56)
601 to 606 ("long-nose")

Hill, Sears, Parkes, et al. Then came Dan Gurney with a V-8 and the Ford Lotus Cortina.

Genuine ex-factory-supported cars are valuable and worth it. Historic racing today dictates a Jaguar sedan revival.

THE XJ12 COUPE

British Leyland, then in control of Jaguar Cars, promoted a race program for the XJ12C in 1976 and 1977. It wasn't altogether successful but the cars are most interesting and worth a second look. They were fast but they didn't last. Direct factory involvement wasn't visible, for the cars were prepared by Broadspeed, a well-known (and highly regarded) race shop, but lack of development time and money hampered things. British Leyland politics played their part too.

No glory this time but considerable experience with the big V-12 for all concerned.

THE LIGHTWEIGHT E-TYPE

The six-cylinder E-type production cars were raced almost from the word go—April 1961 saw Graham Hill win at Oulton Park first time out. By far the majority of E-types on the track were such, anything from "box stock" to factory developed, wind-tunnel tested, lightweight steel monocoque, wide angle D-type cylinder head rockets. But then there were the factory light Lightweights, with alloy center section monocoque of which a dozen were made. Of these true Lightweights, Briggs Cunningham had three and he did well. These cars were genuinely successful and continue to be so in historic racing.

These cars are valuable and both interesting and confusing because there are replicas around and retro-fit cars with Lightweight parts (including monocoque).

Definitely in the mold of the Ferrari 250GTO and Aston Martin DB4GT Zagato.

E-TYPE SERIES THREE V-12 RACERS

The racing heritage of Jaguar which extended across more than four decades has never really died. The factory, while declining to enter racing after 1956, felt the aerodynamic lines and V-12 engines should produce victories. The factory did assist in the preparation of several "ultralight" racing XK-E models. Under separately endorsed projects in the seventies, Lee Mueller road raced a V-12 roadster in the US that was prepared by Joe Huffaker. Bob Tullius and Bob Fuerstenau of Group 44 drove a heavily modified Series Three V-12 roadster. Their car produced the first victories for the marque in fifteen years in direct racing competition at the manufacturers trophy level. British Leyland (now the parent of Jaguar Cars) provided extensive technical assistance for these efforts and, in turn, reaped valuable technical information on body and chassis design and drivetrain performance.

THE XJ 13

Prior to the introduction of the XJ-S, the design group at Jaguar studied the possibilities of building a mid-engined racing car which would compete with the exotic cars being produced on the Continent by Ferrari and Lamborghini. The designers ultimately built a trial two-place roadster and began to test it with the prototype in the late-sixties. The XJ 13, as it was officially known, attained 161.6 mph on the enclosed track at MIRA, a lap record which still stands. It was damaged in a tire-failure spin while testing the four-camshaft engine that ultimately spawned the Series Three V-12 engine. The car was restored, but the ultimate production decision was in favor of the XJ-S.

XJ-S RACING

Bob Tullius and Group 44 had developed a close liaison with Jaguar (more specifically British Motor Company, British Leyland and, ultimately, Jaguar-Rover-Triumph) over the past fifteen years and the evolution of their custom racing efforts to the XJ-S was natural. The Group 44 project was launched in the late seventies and compiled an impressive SCCA (Sports Car Club of America) and Trans-Am record while winning the Driver's Championship twice and the Manufacturers Championship once. Much of the promotional effort of JRT was well-founded and the popularity of the cars grew. The record of the XJ-S (as modified) is still being established.

THE XJRS-5

The XJ 13 stirred a great deal of excitement in Jaguar enthusiasts who longed for a truly competitive, high-speed car. Subsequent events allowed their ardor to cool throughout the seventies, only to be rekindled in 1981 with the Group 44 project car developed for the International Motor Sports Association's 1982 season. This car, designed for endurance racing, garnered a third place on its first outing. Its true merit is being tested as this book goes to press and it has been very competitive during the 1983 racing season in spite of two mishaps.

THE XJR-6, XJR-7 AND XJR-8

In early 1987, Group 44 drew back on its racing commitments and much of the Jaguar glory was being achieved in the European (Group C) equivalent of IMSA Phototype competition in the United States. The new standard bearer that emerged in 1986 was the Silk Cut Team which finished third in both the Drivers and Teams sections of the World Sports Car Championship.

In 1987, John Watson and Jan Lammers inaugurated the season by winning at Jarama (near Madrid) with the Silk Cut XJR-6. This V-12-powered car achieved 700 hp at 7000 rpm, and followed with a second Spanish "reign" with a win at Jerez.

These custom performers are showing the definite positive effects of a continuous development plan and winter practice.

It should not take long for the effects to trickle into the IMSA circuit. The latest model being tested is a so-called sprint car, the XJR-8. This new-found success should heighten interest in all Jaguar activities.

The XK-SS. Note short nose from early D-type styling. *Road & Track* photo.

XK-SS

ENGINE
Type: in-line 6-cylinder
Bore x Stroke, mm: 83x106
Displacement: 3442 cc
Valve Operation: twin overhead camshaft
Compression Ratio: 9:1
Carburetion: 3 twin-choke Weber
Bhp (Mrf): 250

CHASSIS & DRIVETRAIN
Transmission: 4-speed synchromesh
Rear Suspension: independent
Gear Ratio: 3.5, 4.5, 5.8, 7.6:1
Front Suspension: independent
Frame: monocoque

GENERAL
Wheelbase, inches: 90⅝
Track, inches: 51½
Brakes: Dunlop disc
Tire Size, front and rear: 6.50x16
Wheels: alloy disc with center lock
Body Builder: Jaguar Cars Ltd.

Chassis Serial Numbers:
XKSS 701 to XKSS 769 (not in numerical sequence), only 18 units known to have been produced

This concours-winning, racing XK 120 demonstrating the racing windscreens was photographed in Ohio. *Jaguar Journal* photo.

Special ultralight racing model of the XK-E created by the factory. This frequent winner is in the Harrah's Automobile Collection. Author photo courtesy Harrah's Automobile Collection.

The XJ 13 prototype which was a mid-engine engineering exercise. (Only one was built.) Andrew Whyte photo.

XJ12C coupe modified for racing. *Jaguar Journal* photo.

XK 140 roadster modified for racing (1982) with alloy wheels, roll bar cage and front airflow dams. This car, owned and prepared for racing by Bob Smiley, was driven by him to the New England C-Production championship in 1981 at the age of 27! Author collection.

An XK 120 roadster prepared for racing by Bob Smiley. Author collection.

XJRS 5 is being successfully raced in the US as this book goes to press. *Jaguar Journal* photo.

Racing XJ-S of Group 44. Bob Stone collection.

Bob Tullius braking hard at Lime Rock in 1974. This Series Three roadster was modified for SCCA class racing. Jaguar Cars, Inc., photo.

The Jaguar motorcar company was born in the act of "customizing" other cars, and it is logical to anticipate variations in Jaguar design, engines and chassis based on the popularity of the XK series. The beauty of line was hard to improve upon and the engine was reliable.

However, special cars did appear. Design variations were basically "one-off" cars which were produced by major design studios on the European continent. Zagato, Vignale and Bertone, who were among the leading coach designers of the time all tried their hand at improving Lyons' lines.

Race variations, better categorized as "limited productions," were combinations of Jaguar components with those of other manufacturers (such as Jaguarette, Jaguaria, HK cars and the LGS cars). The builders sought personal racing advantage and varying degrees of success were achieved. However, the desirability of these cars is high and all rate as collector items. HWM cars, Alta-Jaguars and Lister-Jaguars all achieved success in the early fifties and some measure of notoriety in the professional racing world. Lister-Jaguars became widely known in the late fifties and were campaigned in England into the mid-sixties.

The Cooper-Jaguar, the Tojeiro-Jaguar and the RGS-Atalanta-Jaguar all married Jaguar engines to varying transmission-frame combinations and clothed them in fiberglass shells. Most had aerodynamic and various road-handling problems which could be easily solved by resculpturing the fiberglass. All qualify as collector items with varying degrees of desirability.

In the United States, the demand for completely forgiving reliability, which could be serviced at the local garage, led enterprising mechanics to replace the slightly temperamental dohc six-cylinder engine with a more tolerant American V-8. Many of these conversions exist and new ones are being produced today. The prospective buyer should be advised that Jaguar has never, I repeat, *never*, offered a production V-8 engine. However, Daimler did offer a V-8 and at least one source says that a few Mark II sedans were equipped with Daimler V-8 engines.

During the decade of the seventies, with the escalation of prices for the classic automobile, "replicars" made their appearance. The perusal of any current car magazine will note multiple advertisements for completed cars or kits that can be assembled and placed over a Volkswagen or Porsche chassis and engine.

Total accuracy of replication (rebuilding to original specifications) demands a significant price but is available. Authenticity and price thereafter drop together.

In 1976, two manufacturers (Lynx Motor Company and Deetype Replicas Ltd.) built repro of the D-type for a modest $24,000. The chassis and suspension were basically E-type and fitted with hand-crafted D-type bodies.

One of the early replicar entries was the Westwinds Panther J-72 produced in England in the early seventies. Utilizing many Jaguar components, an attempt was made to duplicate the SS 100 with some artistic and surprising commercial success. The J-72 upgraded many features, regularly adding to the motoring comfort and safety. Antique & Classic Automotive, Inc., introduced a similar SS 100 duplication in 1982.

Recently, Eagle Coachworks brought an XK-120G to the marketplace. It demonstrated a remarkable similarity to the original XK 120 model except for the XK 140 grille style and late-model wire wheels.

Road & Track reported in its October 1982 issue that Kentish House in Vancouver, British Columbia, Canada, was bringing out a replica of the XK-E for $42,000. Tony Hogg, the late editor-in-chief of the magazine, stressed that this is a "re-manufactured" car (according to the Canadian company) and, therefore, one questions whether it is truly a replicar or an expensive commercially available restoration. The buyer is again cautioned to ascertain the authenticity of a car if it is indeed being offered as an authentic vehicle, as some of the replicas look very much like the real thing.

The reader is also cautioned about counterfeit cars. These reproductions, usually of rare and therefore highly desirable models (e.g., SS 100, C-type and D-type, XK-SS) are quite close to the original. The authenticity of all such offerings should be verified.

PARTS & SERVICE SOURCES

Although far from complete and totally untested, the following list can get a novice restoration under way. Citation in this list does not presume endorsement.

E-Jag
P.O. Box J
Carlisle, Massachusetts 01741
   A magazine listing parts, repair shops and services which owners have recommended. Although caution must always be exercised, these will frequently be a good starting point.

Oldham & Crowther
27-31 Ivatt Way
Westwood Industrial Estate
Peterborough PE3 7PH
England
   Leading specialists in Jaguar restoration, race preparation, panel and trim manufacture, parts, reconditioned engines etc.

British Auto Interiors
1555 Elm Street
Manchester, New Hampshire 03101
(603) 622-1050

Bill Tracy
3179 Woodland Lane
Alexandria, Virginia 22309

Vintage Jaguar Spares (pre-XK only)
Robert C. Brosen
7804 Billington Court
Oxon Hill, Massachusetts 20744

Bassett's Jaguar Parts & Interiors
P. O. Box 145
Peace Dale, Rhode Island 02881

Rhode Island Wiring Service, Inc.
P. O. Box 24
Kingston, Rhode Island 02881

RECENT PRICES

For reference only, I have included a review with sample prices. Each figure represents an estimated, composite figure I derived from the classified advertisements of *E-Jag, Road & Track, The News and Technical Bulletin* and *The New York Times.*

The reader should understand that these are "asking" prices, not actual sale prices. Often the price is lower due to bartering.

These price estimates do not include any replicars, reproductions or conversions.

(Absence of data indicates only rarity of that model in the sales market.)

Data collected from June to December 1982.

	High	Average	Low
SS 100	45,000	28,000	–
SS Jag (prewar)	9,000	–	–
(postwar)	–	5,000	–
MARK V			
DHC	55,000	16,500	–
Sedan	15,000	9,500	5,000
XK120			
Roadster	20,000	13,500	7,500
FHC	18,000	–	9,500
DHC	55,000	11,000	4,500
XK140			
Roadster	17,000	15,000	12,500
FHC	9,000	5,000	3,000
DHC	16,000	11,000	3,000
XK150 and XK150S			
FHC	25,000	12,000	8,000
DHC	14,000	8,500	4,000
Roadster	27,000	6,500	4,000
C Type	–	–	–
D Type	–	200,000	–
XKE			
Series One and Series One and One-Half			
Roadster	20,000	12,000	6,000
FHC	14,500	7,000	2,500
2+2	9,500	6,500	2,500
Series Two			
Roadster	17,000	11,500	5,000
FHC	11,500	7,500	5,000
2+2	14,000	9,500	5,000
Series Three			
Roadster	23,000	16,000	14,000
2+2	13,000	10,000	7,000
MARK VII	20,000	9,000	3,500
MARK VIII	–	5,500	–
MARK IX	20,000	–	–
MARK X	–	8,500	–
420G	–	2,900	–
2.4	6,500	5,000	3,500
3.4	15,000	7,000	2,000
3.8 Mark II	10,000	7,000	2,000
3.8S	7,000	5,000	3,500
420	–	3,000	–
XJ 6 and XJ 6L			
1969-76	10,000	6,000	3,500
1977-82	24,500	19,000	17,000
Vanden Plas	32,000	–	–
XJ 12 and XJ 12L	17,000	11,000	7,000
XJ 6C	25,000	11,500	8,500
XJ 12C	19,000	10,000	8,000
XJ-S	18,000	14,000	10,000

Data collected from December 1986 to June 1987.

	High	Average	Low
SS 100	82,500	45,000	32,000
SS (prewar)	80,000	57,000	38,000
(postwar)	25,000	17,000	12,500
Mark V			
DHC	32,000	20,000	12,000
Sedan	28,500	12,500	7,250
XK 120			
Roadster	32,500	17,500	10,000
FHC	16,000	12,000	7,500
DHC	30,000	18,500	12,000
XK 140			
Roadster	19,500	15,000	–
FHC	17,000	15,000	8,000
DHC	24,500	18,500	8,500
XK 150			
Roadster	22,500	15,500	9,500
FHC	17,500	14,500	8,000
DHC	20,000	14,000	8,000
"S"	22,500	13,500	8,000
C-Type		45,000	
D-Type		200,000	
XKE			
Series One and One-Half			
Roadster	24,000	15,000	12,000
FHC	20,000	12,000	8,000
2+2	12,500	10,500	7,000
Series Two			
Roadster	22,500	15,000	10,000
FHC	17,500	12,500	7,500
2+2	10,500	8,750	7,500
Series Three			
Roadster	37,500	22,000	17,500
2+2	20,000	14,500	10,000
Mark VII	14,000	–	6,000
Mark VIII	18,000	–	3,500
Mark IX	20,000	8,500	3,000
Mark X	15,000	10,000	8,500
420G	–	6,750	–
2.4	–	5,000	–
3.4	7,000	6,000	2,500
3.8 II	17,500	6,500	4,500
3.8 S	–	6,000	4,000
420	9,000	7,200	6,000
XJ 6			
Series I	9,500	5,500	3,800
Series II	19,000	7,500	5,500
Series III	35,000	22,500	18,000
Coupe	20,000	13,500	8,900
XJ 12			
Series II	14,000	12,000	9,500
Coupe	16,500	15,000	11,500
XJ-S			
Coupe	25,000	18,000	10,000
Cabriolet	35,900	25,000	–
Convertible	–	–	–

CLUBS

Jaguar Clubs of North America, Inc.
600 Willow Tree Road
Leonia, New Jersey 07605
   Sponsored by Jaguar Cars, Ltd., and assists more than forty regional and special-interest Jaguar clubs.

Jaguar Touring Club
Richard Bowman, President
71 Route 25A
Smithtown, Long Island
New York 11787
   A group of devotees of older Jaguars.

Classic Jaguar Association
Jack Rabell, President
2860 W. Victoria Drive
Alpine, California 92001
   A national organization devoted to the prewar and early postwar Jaguars. Its publications are full of technical information.

Jaguar Drivers' Club
Jaguar House
18 Stewart Street
Luton
Beds LU1 2SL
England

XK Club
Phil Henshall, Secretary
46 Toll Bar Road
Great Boughton
Chester, England

RECOMMENDED READING

BOOKS

In the past five years, a plethora of books have examined Jaguars from most viewpoints. The following books are readily available. It is a selected group to stimulate your interest and to provide reference materials.

Frostick, Michael. *The Jaguar Tradition*. London: Dalton Watson Ltd., 1973.

Harvey, Chris. *E-Type: End of an Era*. New York: St. Martins Press, 1977.

Lord Montagu of Beaulieu. *Jaguar*. South Brunswick: A. S. Barnes and Company, 1967.

Skilleter, Paul. *Jaguar Sportscars*. Somerset, England: Foulis, 1975.

———. *The Jaguar XKs*. London: Motor Racing Publications, Ltd., 1981.

———. *Jaguar Saloon Cars*. Somerset, England: Foulis, 1982.

———. *The Jaguar Sedans*. London: Motor Racing Publications, Ltd., 1981.

Whyte, Andrew. *Jaguar: The History of a Great British Car*. Cambridge: Patrick Stephens Ltd., 1980.

DATA MONOGRAPHS

These are collections of data and tests conducted by acknowledged technical experts. These may prove beneficial to the novice buyer by providing detailed technical information not available in a more accessible form.

Jaguar (SS) Cars 1931-1937
Jaguar (SS) Cars 1937-1947
Jaguar Cars 1948-1951
Jaguar Cars 1951-1953
Jaguar Cars 1954-1955
Jaguar Cars 1955-1957

(Note: Some of these have been combined into hard-cover collections)
Published by Brooklands Books Distribution, Surrey, England.

Road & Track Road Tests

Jaguar tests have been collected and are available through the publisher.

Road & Track Magazine
1499 Monrovia Avenue
P.O. Box 1757
Newport Beach, CA 92663

MAGAZINES—DEVOTED TO JAGUARS

Periodic publications that feature Jaguars exclusively are few but their quality is excellent and the interested Jaguar owner is urged to consult their pages.

E-Jag — Published in the Boston area originally as a newsletter for owners of New England E-types, this full-color quality magazine has embraced all models and has become a significant source of useable information.

E-Jag Publications
P.O. Box J
Carlisle, MA 01741

The Jaguar Journal — Published by British Leyland Ltd. in cooperation with the Jaguar Clubs of North America. It provides general information about Jaguar products, marketing and statistics. In most instances, the information relates to new models. Possesses a limited want-ad section.

The Jaguar Journal
600 Willow Tree Lane
Livonia, NJ 07866

The Jaguar Driver and *The XK Driver* — Both are published in Great Britain. Both began as newssheets for their respective organizations but have included sufficient general information to be worthwhile subscriptions.

The Jaguar Driver
Magpie Publishing Company
23 Thames
Walton-on-Thames
Surrey, England
The XK Driver
Richard Woodley, Editor
58 Windsor Avenue
Radyr, Glam, England

The News and Technical Bulletin — Published by the Classic Jaguar Association. Although this is a club newsletter oriented to prewar models, it contains a wealth of information about most collectable Jaguars. The technical tips and the advertisements (frequently reproductions of business cards) for restoration parts make this newssheet a "must" subscription for the serious Jaguar owner or restorer of older Jaguars.

The News and Technical Bulletin
Classic Jaguar Association
Mason Roe, Editor
Route 2, Box 43
Templeton, CA 93465

Jags Unlimited — merged with *Jaguar Marque* to become *Jaguar International Magazine*.
1306 S Pope
Benton, IL 62812

Most Jaguar clubs, whether local or regional, publish a newsletter for their members at regular intervals, and most welcome the opportunity to circulate nationally. Your interest, reading time and pocketbook are the only limits. In addition, the quality of their subject material, writing, photography and reference material will vary but are usually good.

MAGAZINES—GENERAL INTEREST

Road & Track — Probably the premier national monthly publication for the auto enthusiast. The "Road Tests" have provided consistent and accurate evaluations of performance, styling, durability and desirability. Has an extensive and usually honest want-ad section, which lists three to ten Jaguars per month.
Road & Track Magazine
1499 Monrovia Avenue
Newport Beach, CA 92663

Car and Driver — An evolution from *Sports Cars Illustrated*, seems to emphasize high performance and "muscle." Has an extensive want-ad section but few Jaguar ads.
Car and Driver
P.O. Box 2770
Boulder, CO 80321

Car Collector and Car Classics — One of several overviews of the car collecting market. Occasional articles and advertisements for Jaguars. A good reference source for general information about car collecting and investing.

Car Collector and Car Classics
Classic Publishing
346 Carpenter Drive, Suite 3
Atlanta, GA 30328

Automobile Quarterly — A hardbound "magazine" devoted to the automotive world. Presents well-researched articles about all aspects of cars. The format and the photography make the subscription well worth the price. Early editions are out-of-print and have become collector items.

Automobile Quarterly
Route 222 and Sharadin Road
Kutztown, PA 19530

Automobile — A new magazine owned by R. Murdoch, edited by David E. Davis, Jr., with glossy-pictured appraisals and articles. The editorial staff includes most of the significant independent automotive writers of our era. Their personalized (opinionated) articles are witty, enjoyable and, above all, accurate. Devoted to high performance cars of all marques and styles. Jaguars included almost monthly.

Automobile
P.O. Box 10997
Des Moines, IA 50340